KNOCKING OUT MY DEMONS

PAUL HUGGINS

Missionaryseed@gmail.com

Published for Paul Huggins by Verité CM Limited,
124 Sea Place, Worthing, West Sussex BN12 4BG
+44 (0) 1903 241975

email: enquiries@veritecm.com
Web: www.veritecm.com

British Library Cataloguing in Publication Data
A record for this book is available from The British Library

ISBN: 978-1-914388-13-2

Printed in the UK

Reviews

This is a sincere, fascinating and gripping autobiography of a man who had been fighting his demons all his life, as we all do, allowing 'Mr Destroyer' to overcome the more pleasant traits of his character, which he had always shown from his early childhood. His Jekyll and Hyde personality, as he calls it in the book, caused him to oscillate between the nice Dr Jekyll and the nasty Mr Hyde.

His boxing, school problems, near-death encounters, and experiences with the drug cartels, police, courts, detention centres, borstal and prisons all make for both alarming and exciting reading.

As we read of his introspective reflection in prison on his life, his conversion to faith, his path to mission in India and the Philippines, we can only admire Paul's tenacity and endeavour to survive, to rid himself of his demons, and become transformed from Mr Hyde to Dr Jekyll. It was a joy to read.

David Henty
Founder and Administrative Director,
SHADES Theatre Company

I have known Paul for many years. We were both born and raised in Hastings, UK, although ten years apart. We were also apprenticed as plumbers and went into local building firms. Later, I got married, had a child and worked on Heating and Ventilation for national swimming pools while Paul became a National Boxing star.

In the early 2000s, we both found ourselves back in Hastings. I, from some years of working in the Middle East and Paul from leaving prison as a Christian. I went into local politics and got elected as a local Councillor, and then after some years, became The Mayor of Hastings. Paul's life changed too in so many ways. He married Bernadette and in 2015 established a charity which imparts Christian values to young children in the Philippines.

His testimonies from a boxer to a criminal to a changed man as a Christian are worth reading. I recommend this book as it shows that with Gods help, good will always win and that all lives have good in them to be found.

Councillor Nigel Colin Sinden
Former Mayor of Hastings 2018-2021

Each chapter has stories which can stand on their own. This book is a very honest, humorous, and detailed narrations of the life of a dear friend. Inspiring, too. This deserves a room in your library.

Alan Marchant
Author and Friend

Contents

Dedication 7

Acknowledgments 9

Preface 11

Part 1:

**EARLY LIFE, TEENAGED ADVENTURES, SCHOOLS,
DETENTIONS, AND BOXING**

1. When and where it all began 15
2. Mum's new man 21
3. Living at Bembrook Road 25
4. Adventure and misadventure 29
5. Tragedies and miracles 35
6. School 41
7. Summer time and the endless adventures it brought 47
8. Discovering Boxing and The West Hill Boxing Club 63
9. My love for Kentucky Fried Chicken and the year 1975 75
10. The crash landing 81
11. Gosport Detention 89
12. Back at home 107
13. My last amateur fight 115
14. The drunken and disorderly boxer 119
15. The launch of my professional boxing career 125
16. Some of my most memorable professional fights 133

Part 2:

DRUG DEALING, CHARITY EVENTS, DEATH ENCOUNTERS, THAILAND, PRISON

17. The beginning of my drug trading and
    smuggling operations with the cartel 153
18. Escape to Thailand 159
19. Deaths of friends and strange encounters 173
20. Downward spiral and continuous brushes with death 181
21. The accusation 191
22. The vicious attack and the shotgun 195
23. The arrest 199
24. The sentencing 203

Part 3:

TRANSFORMATION, THE UPS AND DOWNS IN MY CHRISTIAN LIFE, FINDING THE LOVE OF MY LIFE, AND THE LESSONS OF MY LIFE

25. Awakening by the Holy Spirit 209
26. Free at last and wrestling with temptations 217
27. The miraculous provision through The Entertainer magazine 221
28. An investigative journey to the Holy Land 227
29. A calling to India: My first mission 231
30. A new friend in Malta 237
31. My dream came true 241
32. The lessons of my life from being a child of the devil
    to a child of God 257

    Resources 269
    Epilogue 271

Dedication

For my hometown, Hastings

Acknowledgments

This book would not have been possible without God, who made everything possible. My story is also a story of His goodness, and I thank Him even for the ability to remember the events of my past, often in great detail.

I thank my family, my boxing trainers, the West Hill Boxing Club, boxing colleagues, and supporters, who all added fuel to my fire throughout my boxing days.

My special thanks to my Mum, (long gone), who documented my boxing career through a scrap book and to Hastings and St. Leonard's Observer, which gave detailed reports of some of my boxing bouts.

The past Mayor, present Mayor, authors and friends were kind enough to give their time to read and review the book, and I would particularly like to thank Nigel, Sinden, James Edward Bacon and Alan Marchant.

David Henty not only reviewed but gladly and exhaustively proof-read the book with his ever-competent wife, Julie.

I would also like to thank St. Andrews Church at Fairlight Hastings for allowing access to its church yard, where we took the cover photo of this book. Special mention to The Hastings Kickboxing Academy where we took some practice shots for the cover.

I owe the cover photo to Luke Jones and Bexhill Film Company.

I have made so many friends throughout the years, and some of you are mentioned in this book. Some were not, but it does not mean that you are not valuable in my life. For confidentiality and your privacy, some names are either omitted or changed, but thank you all for being a part of my journey.

I am also touched by your (my friends') eagerness for this book to be completed and for all the offers of help I have received for its marketing.

Finally, my thanks to my wife, Bernadette, for her support and patient hours of reading and editing the manuscript as the book developed.

Preface

I am Paul and this is my story.

I wrote this to inspire you, to give you hope and to keep you going. I want to let you know that, imperfect as we are, there is always a new beginning, a second, even a third chance.

I am ashamed to admit that in the past I have lived a life of wickedness and selfishness, and of fame and of downfall. But my past did not define my present nor my future. In one of the darkest moments in my life, I found hope. As I tell my story of transformation, I want to point you to that hope which has a heartbeat to the truth, either long supressed or deprived. To the truth, which knocked out my demons, and continues to knock out my demons. To the truth of God, His Word (the Bible) and to the salvation, which is available to those who choose to believe. *"For I am not ashamed of the gospel, because it is the power of God that brings salvation to everyone who believes: first to the Jew, then to the Gentile."* Romans 1:16. As I tell my story, it is my prayer that you may realise that there is something greater and better than the lies and deceptions, which the world through temporary pleasures makes you believe. And as I tell my story, and you see yourself in the chapters of my life, I hope you realise that it is not too late for Jesus to turn your life around. God's plan is bigger than our shameful past.

You are valuable. You are unique. You have a purpose. You can make a difference. Most importantly, you are loved. Loved by your Creator. Loved by Jesus with a Perfect Love. Do not let the world have you believe otherwise. *"So, God created man in His own image; in the image of God, He created him; male and female He created them."* (Genesis 1:27). Your value begins with the fact that you have been made in the image of your Creator. *"Your eyes saw my unformed body; all the days ordained for me were written in your book before one of them came to be."* (Psalm 139:16). Your Creator also promised you a life of purpose and meaning, if you seek Him.

It took me years to understand my identity in Jesus. Looking back, if I knew, accepted and understood the Truth I know now, I would have lived differently. I would have FEAR and REVERENCE to the One who created me. I would have valued my personal relationships and the talents. I would have dealt with my weaknesses with strength and wisdom. But this story would also have been different and it is with great delight that with my past, I could possibly be used to bring hope to the hopeless, especially to the following: a man or a woman who struggles with vices we naturally fall into; to an athlete blinded by his or her own fame and glory; to a criminal blinded by his desire to be rich or driven by pleasures; to a son or a father who seeks to restore relationships with his loved ones; even to a believer in Jesus, who continues to struggle with everyday sin or who is fulfilling the great commission.

I am not an Author and write this with vulnerability. I would apologise if my style is not your preference but I do hope that even if you cannot identify with my life, failings and transformation, that you would, at the very least, be entertained with the recollection of the mundane and light moments of my life. Writing this book also made me realise that there is joy in the simple things in life, in the mundane details of our childhood and even in the recklessness of our youth.

And so, despite my lack of expertise, I share my story and I am sure that you will enjoy this book from cover to cover.

God willing, as you do, it would fulfil my purposes.

May this book find its way to your heart.

PART 1:

EARLY LIFE,
TEENAGED ADVENTURES,
SCHOOLS, DETENTIONS,
AND BOXING.

CHAPTER 1

When and where it all began

I was born in England, on the 15th of July 1961 at Buchanan Hospital. The hospital was located in a historic place, called Hastings, where the battle between the Norman-French, army of William, the Duke of Normandy and the English took place on the 14th October 1066.

Hastings.

I can only imagine that in the maternity ward there was the sound of a spanking going on. It was followed by a loud screeching from a wriggling baby who wasn't very pleased at all, as one big, fat lady, firmly gripped his little feet, and hung him upside down.

She was slapping my sweet little backside, and I was screaming, *"Mum, help me, this is killing me. Let me go! That hurts! How dare you?"*

Nevertheless, there was surely a sense of wonderful joy from Win, my Mummy, as I came into life here on planet earth.

What a relief it must have been for both me and Mum, when I was finally handed into the protective clutches of her bosom. From there, my first little steps into the big wide world started, and opened my eyes to the beginning of the first memory of my childhood at 3 years old.

Like I suppose any normal child, I was clingy. I loved to be in the company of Mum and Dad. Sadly, they separated after I turned two.

Mum and Dad kept me busy with new things, which just appeared like magic from nowhere for hours. But then, from early childhood, especially, when I was left on my own, someone would come along out of nowhere. He is my, not so nice, friend, Mr. Mischief, who I could hear, whispering, "*Ummm, I wonder what this tastes like, or what is this used for, or how can I get into this*?"

Oh, I think no one could have anticipated and expected that my naughtiness could have sprung so early.

Eventually, as you will learn later, Mr. Mischief would turn into Mr. Destroyer who took me into deeper and higher levels of mischief but, before I get ahead of myself, allow me to replay some precious childhood memories.

At 3, I remember the anticipation of my Dad's visits, especially on Saturdays in our little two-bedroom maisonette flat located in Bembrook Road, Hastings. I was always excited, whenever I heard a knock on the door. I knew that it would be my Daddy coming to get me. It was Saturday morning. I knew it was morning time because it was no longer dark. "*Hey, there was light. Wow! Cool.*" I also knew that Dad would take me out for a drive on his lap in his nice, posh Capri car with my hands on the steering wheel.

If I was a good boy and had not steered his car into a wall, he would treat me to something special that we didn't usually get from Mum.

In those days, times were hard, you see, but Mum did her best and there was always a treat after the 'rag and bone man' had come round and Mum earned a few shillings from some old junk we had lying around. *"He's coming, Mum!"*, I would shout loudly with excitement. I could hear him calling out on his arrival with a bell as big and loud as could be, *"Ring-a-ding ding, Rag 'n' Bone!"* he shouted. He usually came on week days.

But today, it was Saturday again, and Dad's time. As usual, there was a knock on the door. Mum usually lay in on Saturday mornings, because there was no school for my older brother, Tony. Ever since dad left, Mum could not sleep so well, so she said, *"Saturday mornings are for my beauty sleep."* I wondered why she needed a beauty sleep when she always looked beautiful to me.

"Are you there, Paul?" Dad would call through the letter box.

I would rush to the kitchen to fetch a chair, dragging it with pride *"look what I can do, Dad!"*. I would then climb upon it and open the door. Dad would give me a hug and find me some clothes to put on.

Then off, we'd go. My dad, me and my brother, Tony, if he was around that is, on one of our adventures.

Getting older, I could recall some of our numerous poaching expeditions out in the vast, beautiful fields of Sussex with our dogs, the ferrets and often, not so friendly and approving farmers. What a performance we had to go through many times, especially when a farmer would turn up, not so elated at us for being on his land without permission. One of the unforgettable ones, you will read later, ended with us in a police station.

For now, allow me to reflect on how my Dad's absence affected me, growing up. I didn't know exactly the reason why Dad suddenly left home.

But something inside of me died that may well result, as it did in my case, to feelings of insecurity and want. Because of the void, I clung onto my mother like a leech. I had no one else to turn to, anyways. Later on, his absence was replaced by an inner feeling of despair which grew within my inner thoughts, and of loss, of the whys and wherefores. These feelings were aggravated by my dear Mum, who felt hurt and bewildered.

Fortunately, my Mum never alienated us from our Dad and despite the circumstances, I knew that Mum loved Dad and Dad loved us.

Looking back, I am thankful that my Mum was not spiteful nor vindictive.

Sadly, not all women would behave like she did. Perhaps, due to the failed and strained relationships, some women would go hammer and tongs to isolate their children from their fathers. From my experience and perspective, the mother is doing more harm than good to a child who cannot speak up for himself or herself.

Oh well, because of my failures as a father, I may not be qualified to discuss the matter, and I'll carry on with my story.

My mum and my grandparents

Mum and I.

I might have been about four, when I heard Mum and her sister, Aunty Glad talking excitedly in our kitchen about someone named John.

Mum had recently met him at the Travelling Fair which came to Hastings' pilot field, every year on Carnival week. A travelling fair is a fun fair that still, to this day, situates itself every summer at the Oval Summer Fields in Hastings.

We had an old box record player in the kitchen where Mum would put thin, black round plastic discs on, called records and then 'just like magic', a sound would come out of it and a very nice sound too.

Mum loved playing Mario Lanza love songs, Elvis Presley, Buddy Holly, the Beatles, and the likes.

I'm not too sure what song it was, but Mum and Aunty Glad were both dancing around the kitchen with glee, like there was no tomorrow. The kettle was whistling away and from it the steam rose up to the ceiling then came dripping down like rain drops falling from the sky, *"Look Mummy, I said, pointing upwards, it's raining!"*

Mum picked me up in her arms, span me around, then turned the cooker off all-in-one elegant motion. I loved being in the kitchen with my Mum, mainly because of the tit bits I'd get, when she cooked.

It's the little things, isn't it? Apart from major disasters, either brought by our own recklessness or the tough challenges, which life naturally bring, we remember the little things, and the simple pleasures of life which gave us so much joy.

Aunty Glad and Mum were only a couple of years apart in age, and they were almost the same shape and height too, 5'1".

Mum had another sister, named Mary, and two brothers, Vick and Bill.

My nanny, Burt, lived in a nice, big Victorian terraced house that had a scullery. I used to have lots of fun down there, squashing cloths in a metal thingy with four legs. They called it a 'mangle'. It sure did mangle things. We used to take the clothes out to the garden to hang them on the line.

Nan lived with her husband, Grandad Arthur, who was an architect with one leg. They said he caught 'gangrene' and had to have his leg cut off. Whatever 'gangrenes' were, I was afraid to catch them. Grandad Arthur had a special book that he would read me stories from. He called it the Bible.

Nanny Edith and Fred were my Dad's parents, who lived in Churchill Avenue. The house had a big garden with an apple tree in it. I always tried to be a good boy with Grandad Fred and

Grandma, probably because I didn't see them as often as I would have liked. Whatever it was, I felt that my grandparents from both sides loved me, unconditionally.

On occasional summer Sundays, I used to sit with Grandad Fred with my uncles and aunties and watch cricket on their black and white television. I sat and waited with anticipation for Nanny Edith's special apple pie that she would bake with the summer time apples taken from the garden tree.

To be honest, it was a treat, even a luxury to enjoy homemade cooking from my grandparents as Mum wasn't the best cook in the world. Maybe, because she was so busy with us, that normally meant we would eat convenient meals from the tins. Mum was an expert at Sunday dinners though. Sunday roast was our highlight of the week as far as dinners were concerned, and we even had a pudding on Sundays. Sunday was just like the old Charles Dickens films, *"Push 'n' Pull it; you've got to pick a pocket or two... on guard... forks at the ready"*.

I loved going to see both my grandparents, and quickly got to know who I could get away with, playing up with the most.

CHAPTER 2

Mum's new man

Stepdad John.

So, the man my Mum met in the fair eventually became my Stepdad.

John was the spit and image of Freddie Mills, the British world light heavyweight champion in the late 1940s. John was about 5 feet 10ins tall with thick dark curly hair and a square jaw to match. Stepdad John was with us for the rest of his life until he died of cancer not long into his sixties.

John was a strong and able man who could fix just about anything around the house. He loved collecting things, too. He collected anything that he thought had a shine to it. Mum used to call him a "magpie". He loved his tea, did our John. Mum said, "*He must have been a teapot in another life.*"

Initially, I was jealous of John.

Even with his good intentions, I remained a selfish, insecure, and jealous little boy, who did not want to share my Mum. It meant my clinginess with Mum was so bad that I hardly ever noticed my older brother, Tony. I only wanted Mum. Perhaps, it was also because Tony was 9 years older than I was. And so, at such a young age of 4, I did my best to ruin everything for Mum and John.

I could only cringe, as I recall how nasty, and such a horrible brat I was then.

I wondered to myself, *"What is this strange man doing in our house?".*

But John persevered to win my affection, first with sweeties.

Every Friday, after John had finished a hard week's work in the building game, and traveling here and there to settle with Mum, I would wait for him at the yard gate. When I spotted him, I was so pleased to see him, as weird as it sounds.

I knew he would have some sweets for me.

However, the 'pleasure from the sweeties' did not last very long. When he started acting like my real Dad and a partner to my Mum, my mind and Mr. Mischief went haywire with *"Hey Mr., I don't mind you making us all happy and bringing home lovely things and taking us to really nice places, but no way are you telling me what to do, and there is no way you will be sleeping in the same bed as my Mum. No way, José."*

My irrational jealousy even went as far as this: one Friday night, Mum and John both went out for some singing and dancing in the Old Town. I found my Mum's knitting wool, unwound a long length off, and then tied one end to my Mum's bedroom door handle and the other end to my wrist. I then fell asleep, probably thinking 'you won't get past me'.

It worked too. I was awoken by my arm being pulled as the door was opened to Mum's bedroom. There wasn't a light on, so Mum didn't see the wool attached to her bedroom door. I jumped out of bed and just would not have any of it. I played up rotten until John had to sleep on the sofa.

Another time, I threatened to jump out of my bedroom window. I was literally hanging on by my fingertips, after being rescued, and a backside slapping to try and teach me a lesson, which never worked!

John had to make some gadgets, so I couldn't open the windows, not only for my own safety, but for Mum's peace of mind.

When I got a bit older, I learned to run away. John, possibly using reverse psychology, got used to it and told me every time, *"Okay then, bye-bye Paul. See you at tea time."* It became like a running joke because I used to come back, anyways. Skinny as I was, I could not and did not let myself grow hungry.

Regrettably, as the months went by, Mum and John were forced 'by my abnormal possessive behaviour' to sleep in separate rooms.

Thank goodness for them, *"Where there's a will, there's a way,"* and one year later, my youngest brother Dean was born. And it finally made sense why my Mum was getting fatter and fatter as the weeks and months went by. I thought it was because she was eating all the pies, chocolates, cakes and puddings.

I eventually grew to accept my dear Stepdad for the hardworking man that he was and the kind man that my Mum found that he was.

Dean was a twinkle in my Mum's and John's eyes. I was thrilled to have a new baby brother. Dean had loads of ginger hair with freckles all over his little face and didn't look as big and as annoying as Tony. Dean made a lot of noise though. I remember he was often squawking like mad. *What an attention seeker! Or was he just plain starving?* Like most babies are.

Oh well, I am happy that it all turned out nicely in the end for me and John and that things changed for the better for us when John came into our lives.

Our view at Bembrook Road.

CHAPTER 3

Living at Bembrook Road

Growing up in No. 213 Bembrook Road now with John was special. The maisonette was our first council house. Most of the houses in the surrounding area were built just before the Second World War and had good, steady all-round craftsmanship.

Like many neighborhoods in Hastings, we face stunning views of the East hill, and green fields. Most treasured though were fond memories with my friends who lived in the neighborhood and our elderly neighbors, as well. Allow me to introduce you to some of them with emphasis on how our shared lives enriched each other.

The 'Bembrook Road Gang' consisted of Philip Baker and his sisters, Dave Lelliott, the Ballards, and there were two lots of the Ballards, then the Mephams, the Bacons, the Hattons, the Gibbs, the Barbreys, the Terrells, the Bentons and the Sherrys. Then around the corner were the Marshs and the Skeltons. They were all bigger families than ours and some of them had up to 8 or 9 kids. Bred like rabbits, as commonly described.

Our next-door neighbours were Ernie and Vera, a lovely, always smartly dressed couple, who were probably in their forties then. They owned a grocery store just around the corner in a street or road called Mount Pleasant. Ernie was always good for some groceries on account. On account meant that Mum paid after the 'rag and bone man' had been around.

Then there was the upstairs block too, where Chris and his Mum, Pat Meachen, lived.

Whenever I saw Pat, I always addressed her with *"Hello, Miss Meachen."*

We had respect for our elders in those days. Pat was our playground supervisor at Mount Pleasant Infant School. She also looked after all the much-needed jumble sale materials handed in by parents, which were sold for school books and other much needed school equipment. She was a kind, strong woman, who could roll her sleeves up and did just about anything in the school grounds. She even climbed over the school fence to get our lost balls back.

Our courtesy, especially mine, did not go unnoticed. We used to get a dear little bottle of milk during our morning play time session, and it was Miss Meachen who handed out the bottles. Miss Meachen always made sure that I got one of the spare leftover bottles.

She would ask with her beaming smile, *"Would you like another bottle, Paul?"*

"Yes please Miss, thank-you", I would say, as pleased as punch.

Her son Chris was a good bloke too. If needed on a Friday night, and if he wasn't busy, he would come down and babysit for us. I liked Chris. He was a gentle giant in my eyes. He used to keep reptiles, frogs, lizards, mice and exotic kinds of fishes and the likes. I, on the other hand, kept a mouse. Chris would sometimes take me to his house to see his beloved collection.

One time our 'Bembrook road gang' caught this huge grass snake from the grass banks beside the railway lines down at the Ore Village Railway Station, where the snakes would bask in the sun. After catching it with our bare hands, we brought it to our front yard and let it wander around the grass. It slithered around so fast, we couldn't catch it.

I hurriedly went and got Chris, *"Quick, Chris! come and see, we've caught a grass snake!"* I said excitedly.

He came and looked. By this time, all the neighbours were out, very curious.

"He might want something to eat." I exclaimed, with fiendish joy. *"Shall I go and get him my pet mouse, Chris?"*

Quite prepared to sacrifice my dear little mouse friend was something I didn't think twice about.

Without even waiting for Chris to reply, I went and fetched it, but the snake wasn't interested in my mouse. Chris said that grass snakes mostly eat frogs and worms and dead things. I put the mouse back in its cage.

Eventually Chris caught our snake. Only goodness knows what he did with it. But I knew it was in good hands.

Later, we learned that we could sell the snakes for a pound in the Old Town pet shop. A pound was a fair princely sum then.

Growing up in the 60s and 70s translated to outdoor activities and so much fun. We kids never got bored. There was always something to do, other than studying, which, unfortunately, I was not so fond of.

I and my friend, Billy Wallis, who lived across the yard from us, always played together. We made flying saucers with lolly sticks, and folding airplanes with old paper we would get from Ernie and Vera's green-grocer shop. Billy and I used to play for hours. Our front yard seemed so enormous to us that we even played football, much to the annoyance of one of our neighbours, Doris. Sometimes our ball bounced off her window.

"Oh no! "

It was hands on heads in a panic. We would all bolt like rabbits and hide in the washing lines until Billy gave us the all clear. Fortunately, no windows were ever broken, probably because we were so small that the ball rarely lifted off the ground.

Billy's Dad, Jim, on some weekends, would take us down the Old Town for yet another adventure. We would take our buckets at low tide and try to find things creeping around in the Rock 'a' Nore.

Hastings is a coastal town, which meant sea and fishes. If we were really fortunate, sometimes we caught a stray fish, a dab or small bass that didn't make the ebbing tide. On these occasions, Jim would buy us, more often than not, an ice cream. We would even get a fish dinner if we caught enough!

Yep, for us kids, there was always something to do back then and somehow, by hook or by crook, we made sure we had money to spend over the weekend. We had to beg, borrow and, ashamedly, with Mr. Mischief's prodding, as you will learn later, steal.

Then there was Royston and his sister, Marketa. They just lived above Billy's place. I and Marketa would play doctors and nurses, *"You show me yours and I'll show you mine."* We even held hands and kissed when people were watching. When you're five or six, it was all just a bit of innocent fun.

Royston was a good friend too. He was older than me. He was an expert in hunting. Royston was the best snake catcher around. Just opposite Marketa and Royston's door were Joyce and Joe's house.

Joyce worked in the Doctor's surgery, which was just a walking distance. Her husband, Joe, was a giant of a man but softie on the inside. Joe used to take me to the public swimming pool along by Hastings Pier called the White Rock Baths.

He taught me how to swim with some polystyrene floats. After many trials and gulps of chlorinated water, success eventually came. I would always be grateful to Joe for teaching me how to swim.

Learning how to swim proved useful later on with my Stepdad, John, and youngest brother, Dean. Occasionally, we went trammel and gill netting way out at sea to catch fishes with Tush and Oxo.

And so there we were, like one big family at Bembrook Road. People talked with each other, our doors were always open, and everyone knew everybody else's business. If you sneezed, by the time it got to the end of the road, it was chronic bronchitis! Like Chinese whispers, gossip was one of our favourite past times.

Sadly, nowadays, we value our privacy too much. We barely know our neighbours.

CHAPTER 4

Adventure and misadventure

My First Train Journey and my Brother, Tony

When I was five, and before Dean was born, Tony, for whatever misdemeanors or even crimes he committed, was taken into a reform school called Redhill, located in Redhill, Surrey in London. Redhill Reform school was a place that I would later be well acquainted with too myself.

One Saturday, my Mum decided that we would take the train and visit my brother. I was excited as I had never ridden on a train before.

I had watched them go under the bridge though. John would sometimes take me down the 'hundred steps', as they were called, that led to the railway station. Then when a train came along, he would lift me up on to the bridge so I could watch the train as it chugged up to us, then passing directly below. It would billow out puffs and puffs of steam from the engines funnel that engulfed us both for a moment. We would wave to the steam engine men as they passed through.

Oh, what a beauty those steam engine trains were. They were still running on our railways up until 1968, and now look at what we have at present, state of the art, million-mile-an-hour-travel fast trains, which take us to the rest of Europe in two hours and with on-board refreshments to boot.

Where did all the years go by? Literally, like a steam or a puff, evaporating.

After Mum packed our picnic lunch and put our glad rags on, off we trotted.

We eventually arrived at Ore train station, which was about a fifteen-minute walk from where we lived. As John went to buy the tickets, Mum brought me a balloon and a chewy sweet to keep me occupied.

The clock ticked away for what seemed ages. Then at last, the train arrived, *Hoorah! Puff Puff Puff Shhhhhh, Clunk, Pissst!*

Some rattling, screeching and then finally to a halt. *"What was this thing?",* I thought, "blinking heck!"

We were about to climb into the train monsters' belly! *Holy moly! Me! Oh my!"* I was overly excited. I didn't know whether I should run or fly.

"All aboard," said the train conductor.

Mum wobbled to the train, helped on by John. Then, grabbing me by the hand, John hauled me up and into the carriage.

Relieved, I felt safe inside. It looked quite comfortable with green velvety seats to sit on, and hanging nets above where you could put your stuff.

Then I realised, I no longer had my balloon. *"Can I have my balloon, please?"*

John hurriedly ran back to the waiting room shed to get the balloon.

Well-pleased, I settled down nicely. The door was shut and secured by the stationmaster. Then off we chugged, a bit of a shaky start but we were soon going through the tunnel towards Hastings Station.

This was my very first train journey that was about to turn into a nightmare.

The tunnel on the approach to Hastings Station is a short three or four hundred yards in length compared to the 'mile-long tunnel', as it was known to us back then. Now, that tunnel was the mother of all tunnels. It was a tunnel that went in the opposite direction going easterly towards Rye. It was only a few hundred yards from Ore station. The tunnel has a great story later.

It wasn't long before we were at Hastings station. It was busier than at Ore, so we had to wait a few minutes before we chugged off again. The carriages had more people by now. It was getting a bit crowded.

After Hastings Station, came St. Leonard's, then West St. Leonard's and on the stations went until we reached a place called Royal Tunbridge Wells, where John said his family lived.

By this time, I was so bored and asking, *"Are we there yet Mum?"*

"Not yet, sweetheart. It won't be long," said Mum.

The train stopped too long at the busy Royal Tunbridge Wells Station. There were lots of people wandering about, getting on and off, chatting and putting their luggage in what looked like fishing nets above the seats, and so it was.

Now the opportunity arose at having the chance to wander off, unnoticed.

"Let us go and investigate along these train corridors,'" whispered Mr. Mischief.

I noticed people were still getting on and off the train, leaving the doors open for the stationmaster to close.

Then it happened, I wandered away. I ventured further along the carriages and then, to my surprise, as quick as the blink of an eye, I just disappeared!

I slipped straight out of an open door and down onto the platform. Then somehow, only goodness knows how, I continued my fall down between the platform and the train until I found myself on the stony track beside the huge train wheels.

"What on earth was I doing down here? Mum's not going to be pleased", I thought, because my shirt had got dirty.

She would probably say, *"Just look at your shirt, it's filthy."* I stood up and found I couldn't see onto the platform. I could only hear the doors being slammed shut.

Then a whistle blowing, and then the chug clunk of the carriage as it was about to pull off from the station. I waved my dear little arms as far as they could reach and shouted something to a pair of black trousers on legs.

I think I might have even screamed, *"Help!"*

The man looked down and started blowing his whistle like crazy as he shouted, *"Stop! Stop! Stop!"*

The black trousers turned out to be the Stationmaster. He reached down and grabbed both my wrists and gently pulled me up into his arms.

The next thing I can remember was the very nice stationmaster taking me onto the train going from carriage to carriage eventually finding my Mum.

"There!" ' I pointed to my Mum, who was approaching us.

"Where have you been?" Mum said, worriedly.

We sat down. They were talking and my Mum was sort of laughing and crying at the same time. Probably in shock at what she heard from the stationmaster.

John just slowly shook his head.

Mum was forever thankful to the Stationmaster and wrote to him and the railway station, telling them how thankful she was that I was found.

The Redhill

Eventually we arrived at Redhill, Surrey. We got into a car after John shouted, "taxi!". The nice taxi man took us to a place which just so happened to be an institution for naughty boys.

Upon arrival, we walked straight ahead towards these huge iron gates. *"Is this a Castle? Does the Queen live here, Mum?"* I asked.

"No, but you might, if you don't behave."

Well, Mum was right. As 10 years later I would experience the misfortune of spending 6 weeks in this very same place. A place where the clock never seemed to tick.

John banged on the door and we were led to a hall by a smartly dressed, tall man in uniform who was whistling, while swinging some keys on his chain.

Seeing Tony wasn't as much fun as being on the train. As brothers, Tony and I had a lot of falling out and in again, but we love each other dearly.

Tony was pleased to see us though and our presence cheered him up no end.

They had plenty to talk about. I just sat quietly looking around at all the inmates. I wondered why they were all dressed in gray trousers and stripy shirts. It looked odd, like an army camp I'd seen on television.

"Hmmmm, I certainly did not want Mum to leave me in this gloomy place. No way, not today!"

That gave me the motivation to restrain myself from wandering off the train again.

"Such a nice boy, aren't I, Mummy?"

CHAPTER 5

Tragedies and miracles

Life went on at home as normal without Tony but Mum told me he would be back after a couple of months.

Dean, now born and being so small, always slept in Mum's room in his little cot.

One day, Dean kept coughing and choking and crying really, really hard. Mum was so worried that she went next door and got Vera. John was off at work at the Costain's building site, where the new local police station was being constructed.

The next thing I remember was an ambulance turning up, and quickly. Mum and baby Dean drove off in it.

I stayed with Vera. I was delighted because it meant no school for me. I was allowed to play in the yard on my big battery-operated tank that my Dad had bought me.

In the morning, Mum and John came back to fetch me from Vera. I was having some breakfast in Vera's kitchen when Mum began to tell us the story of what had happened.

Dean was taken to the Royal East Sussex Hospital. She said that little Dean seemingly had stopped breathing then turned blue. They called in the church Chaplain and every one began to pray, Mum, John and the nurses.

As they were praying, the colour returned to baby Dean's face. His little heart began to beat. He coughed and then he began to breathe again.

Mum said she believed that they all had witnessed a miracle. Dean was back home with us within a couple of days later. Mum was the happiest ever.

As a Christian, I later read in the Bible that Jesus performed miracles and healed those who believed. During that time, I am certain that my Mum, who would confirm her faith before she died, the Chaplain and the nurses all believed in a God who healed. And so, God performed the miracle.

Soon, Tony was back home too.

However, another tragedy, which to this day I feel so sad about, befell our family. It was a week day and I wondered why John, who never ever missed a day's work, was home.

I could sense that something was amiss or something was not right. My hunches turned out to be true when the police with Tony arrived in our house and they all looked very sad. They went into the kitchen and shut the door.

Mum was crying. They were talking something about the West Hill rocks and my cousin, Clive.

Clive was Aunt Glad's only Son. Tony took Clive for a walk over the West Hill, where Clive wandered off and he strayed too close to the edge of the cliff. I understand that Tony, who liked collecting birds' eggs, was not paying much attention to Clive because he told him to stay away from the edge. Tony trusted that he would do as he was told. And so it was. Tony was after the Herring Gulls eggs, while the curious Clive ventured and fell to his death.

It was a terrible accident, as you can imagine. What followed were months of anguish between us and Aunty Glad but also a glimmer of light and hope.

One night, not long after little Clive's passing, Aunt Glad had a dream, which she vividly narrated to us as if it was real. She said that she saw a soft light at the bottom of her bed. Auntie Glad told us that she could hardly believe what she saw. Standing at the bottom of her bed was Clive!

"He looked like my little angel," Auntie Glad added.

"Is that you, Clive?"

"Yes, Mummy, it's me, Clive. Please don't worry, Mummy, I'm with Jesus now and have so many friends to play with. Jesus is so kind to us."

The miraculous 'dream encounter' healed and kept Aunt Glad going. It gave her new hope. Being a Christian, as were Grandma and Pa, she knows that the Word of God is true. As the Bible tells us (in Matthew 19:14), Jesus himself said, *"Let the little children come to me and do not hinder them, for to such belongs the kingdom of heaven."*

Aunt Glad died in 2018 in her 80s and, because she had faith in Jesus, is reunited with Clive. She left behind her beautiful daughter, Claire, and her grandchildren, Amy and Ryan.

Our Dad.

My Mum had arranged for me and Tony to go visit Dad on a Sunday at his new house that he lived in with his wife, Vale and our half-brother and sister, Nick and Alison. They lived down over the West Hill in Wellington Rd, about half an hour walk from where we were.

Tony would hold my hand as we walked over the hill. We would search for licker sticks on the way to Dad's house. Mum would dress us up in our best clothes. She did her best to make us look smart. I loved going to Dad and Vale's. Nick and Alison had an amazing bedroom with loads of stuff we could play with. Vale cooked really nice dinners too. I would not forget our very special treat, which was tinned Salmon and cucumber sandwiches. Compared to pilchard sandwiches back home, those were real treats.

Dad was a merchant seaman and told us some seafaring stories. He even had some diving equipment. Apparently, when he was learning to dive in the Old Town out in the harbour, his diving friends didn't tell Dad to put on his lead weight diving belt, so he only got down as far as his waist. Everyone had a good laugh. All they could see were Dad's legs waving around in the air! Dad was fine with it. He didn't mind a good laugh even if the laugh was on him. He had some good tricks to play of his own, anyways.

Dad was also renowned for his street fighting skills. I heard many stories that he was good with the head-butt.

One such story was that, one day, there came to town a travelling fair.

There was a boxing booth at the fair for the fairground boxing team that used to take on 'all comers'.

This day, Dad was with his mates at the Oval.

"Come on Ken," said Phil Barker, Dad's friend, *"have a go."*

Not being the type of man to show any fear, Dad took up the challenge but his shots did not make him look good to win. From my own experience, real boxing and street fighting are not synonymous.

Dad then changed his tactic and landed a big head-butt flush on his opponent's forehead. Timber!!!! Down the opponent fell. It was all over.

"Come on, lets run," shouted Phil.

Dad did not bother to get his prize money as they made their quick exit. In my opinion, Dad won by a technical knockout. At least it was technical.

Just a bit of trivia, especially for the boxing fans. Boxing booths have been around for two hundred years. Many great fighters used to earn much of their living from these boxing booths. The likes of two great Welsh fighters, William James, 'Jimmy' Wilde and Tommy Farr come to mind. William James became the

World Flyweight Champion. They called him Jimmy the 'Ghost with the Hammer in His Hand' because he punched more like a welter weight. Tommy Farr, the 'Tonypandy Terror', fought the great World Heavyweight Champion, Joe Louis. He went 15 rounds with Joe.

And so, it seems that I inherited some of Dad's skills in fighting. Guess boxing was in my blood.

Years later, I would box in the Old Town Hastings Carnival day, taking on all comers for a bit of fun and a charity of my choice, as in the photograph:

———

CHAPTER 6

School

Mount Pleasant Infants was my first school. Tony would get me dressed, give me some porridge or, if he felt generous, some corn flakes. Then he would take me down Mount Pleasant Hill, past Ernie's to the school gates. Then off he'd trot to his own school at Priory Road Secondary School.

Early on, I realised I did not like school that much because I could not do as I liked.

I wasn't too keen on Miss Bradshaw either. She was always grabbing and twisting my ears.

Mr. Mischief got the better of me one day as I let off some banger fireworks in her class. Believe it or not, during those days, we could get anything we wanted, especially through our older friends. The explosion almost scared her to death. She wasn't too pleased at all. I had to stand in the corner with my hands on my head until I almost died.

From Mount Pleasant Infant School, it was time to go to a bigger school and this was Elphinstone Primary School.

I was 6 years old then and could now walk to school on my own. There was a 'lollypop lady' on the top of the hill who helped us cross the road safely and also a 'lollypop man' at Elphinstone school gates. We call them 'lollypop people' because they were dressed in yellow jackets and had a long lollypop stick with a sign saying 'STOP'. They were friendly and good at stopping traffic for us. For me they were, and still are to this day and age, unsung heroes.

A year after at 7, Mr. Mischief taught me a new trick, but I utilised it for a good cause. Some mornings, before I left for school and when there was nobody around, I would take a florin, 'a two-shilling coin' from Mum's purse.

I know that there was no excuse for my selfish, thieving behaviour.

Why did I do this? I used the money to buy a bag of doughnuts in a store next to Ernie and Vera's green grocers and hand them out to kids, who I thought were more deprived than me.

Surprisingly, I had some good in me. Mum would later describe me as 'Jekyll and Hyde.'

My Robin Hood stunts did not last very long. Mum discovered my stealing.

I don't know how mum did it, but she came in the kitchen and asked, *"Paul, have you taken two shillings from my purse?"*

I flatly denied the allegation, *"No, Mummy."*

"Yes you have," she insisted.

She took me out to the front yard. Mum got her little hand hoe and proceeded precisely to the spot where I would hide the shillings. I hid them under a little flower bed. She then plucked, 'to my horror', the florin silver coin up into her hand and thrust it straight out in front of me, saying, *"What's this, then?"*

I was gob smacked. Staring wide eyed open mouthed at Mum, totally speechless. I figured that she was not lying when she said she had eyes in the back of her head.

"OK, get your shoes on."

"Now I'm in big trouble," I thought.

We were going to see Mr. West. Mr. West was our Elphinstone School Headmaster.

"This was going to be tricky," I realised, too late.

Mum shut the front door, grabbed my little hand and off we marched down towards the school. My imagination went wild and dreaded what lay ahead. I felt like everybody was looking at me, that the whole world was swallowing me up.

Eventually, we arrived in the school. She almost broke my arm as she dragged me hurriedly to Mr. West's office.

Mr. West was a tall man who always wore a dark suit, like what you wear at funerals. Today, I felt it was my funeral.

"Come along little man," said Mum. Mum knocked on Mr. West's door.

"Hello. Mrs. Huggins, what can we do for you?"

Mum told him about my stealing. I stood there, feeling sorry for myself and petrified. Mr. West's wooden desk began to resemble a coffin. My imagination could hear the morning Assembly singing, *"I'm on my way to heaven!"*

Well, that is what it sounded like.

I bowed my head and whispered, *"Dear Lord, please help me."*

Years later, unexpected spontaneous prayers would also save me from some consequences of my foolish actions. The fact that we pray to a God we do not know or believe in is an irony, but it feels like the most natural thing to do in desperate situations.

Now that I am a Christian, I realised that deep down, though we choose to deny, even dispute and reject God, at the very least most of us acknowledge the existence of a God who could save us and who could do the impossible for us.

"Ummm, come here, Paul," said Mr. West in a gentle way. *"We need to have a wee talk."*

After explaining all the fundamentals of theft, he then said, what I would never forget, *"If you want two shillings, little fella, you come and ask me."*

And that was it. I received no punishment, just an offer of help.

"Thank you, Mr. West."

I joyfully skipped to the Assembly Hall. Just in time for my favourite song, *"Dance, dance wherever you may be. I am the Lord of the dance, said He and I lead you all, wherever you may be, I lead you all to the dance said He . . ."*

I learned some things in Elphinstone, although not much, and made new friends.

My school report mostly said, *"Paul could do so much better, if only he would put more effort into his studies, instead of trying to win first prize as the classroom clown!"*

True enough, to this day, I regretted it that I never exerted effort in my studies.

The only excuse I could think of for my dismal academic performance in school was this: I liked being a clown, especially with all the attention that came from being so silly. It was my own safe, little entertaining world, where I could delight in all the attention.

But I always looked forward to our Psychical Education classes with Mr. Yorkstone. Mr. Yorkstone had wavy ginger hair, with a kind tanned smiling face that adorned a moustache. He was a sturdy, flamboyant man who always wore colourful tracksuits, even in the winter.

I guess academics and later on athletics did not mix, as far as I was concerned.

It is refreshing that these days school athletes need to commit and are encouraged to do well in school. I cannot over emphaze the importance of valuing formal education or even learning a skillful trade. Both are potential fallbacks, in case you fail in athletics or you lose your value in the sports you choose a career out of.

Depending on the weather, we would run around on the playing fields, usually playing football, or being trained for our summer fete games. During the latter, our Mums and Dads would come on a Sunday afternoon to cheer us on in the three-legged races, track and field, long jumping and the likes. There were always stalls to buy some nice homemade cakes, jams and honey with bric-a-brac stalls too.

I was so skinny and small that Mum often exclaimed, *"If a gust of wind had of come along, I would have been blown away."*

Despite my size, I loved the competitions. I was very competitive then and would always give the big boys a good run for their money, so to speak. I would finish either second or third.

Every weekday we would go into the Assembly Hall so the teachers could tick off our school attendance register. Then Mr. Reed would play the piano and we would sing good old-fashioned, Christian hymns.

More often than not, during summer times, I and my best friends, John Terell, David Quincy and John Hansel were the last students to turn up in school.

On our way to class, we would venture into the fields to look for mice, lizards and slow worms. We would catch them, stroke them for a while, then let them go.

Sometimes I'd take a lizard to school to make the girls scream. I got a slapped backside' from a teacher for being naughty. We would also play hide and seek and 'kiss chase' with the girls.

Just before the final afternoon bell, the teacher would instruct us to tidy up, and we made sure that everything was in its right place for the next morning's lessons.

As soon as the bell went, there was a stampede for the door, followed by our teacher shouting, "*Slow down, Huggins,*" which I did until I got out of site.

CHAPTER 7

Summer time and the endless adventures it brought

Nearly 8 years old and some of the Bembrook gang had moved out to bigger and posher houses.

I was glad I had the two Johns, David, the Mephams and the Ballards to play with during the summer, and I would meet up with them.

We would continue our catching expedition in the fields next to the railway lines. We would catch butterflies, lizards, mice and just about anything that moved really.

We were fascinated with insects and animals and were mesmerised as we watched them, often very, very closely.

The field ants would build their nests, and they looked like huge mounds of dry sand and dirt. I noticed that ants were industrious little creatures, which walk to and from their nests, carrying all kinds of things like sticks, grubs and dead insects. There were black ants and there were red ants. The red ants were more aggressive than the black. They refuse to be in the same nests, and had their own territories. Ants had little nips which could sting you, as I found out, painfully, when we were scurrying around in the long grass.

I felt tired and wanted to sit down for a rest. *"What's that itching?"* I wondered.

And I felt sharp nips on my backside. I looked down at my shorts and screamed, *"Ahhh!"* The ants were feasting on my backside, crawling everywhere. I leaped and ran for the bumpy track that led to the railway bridge. I was jumping up and down, slapping myself all over. *"Ahhh!"* I screamed again.

David and John were watching me, rolling around on their backs and laughing their heads off. I spotted a puddle of water in the track and I instinctively plunged into it rolling around trying to get the ants off me.

"I'm going home," I exclaimed to my friends. I then ran off up the hill as fast as I could go, urgently needing a bath and a cuddle from Mum.

I didn't normally like getting in the bath, but that day I was grateful I had one.

We also had fun watching the grass tractor man cut the grass, out in the fields.

After he had cut all the grass, we would have to wait for a day or so for the sun to dry them out. Using the dried grass, we then built the walls, only about two or three feet high, for our straw houses.

The roof was made of corrugated metal roofing sheets, which we got from Tin Town.

Tin Town was an area over the railway bridge. It was called Tin Town because during the war, the houses built especially for the homeless were constructed with corrugated metal sheets. As the houses were demolished, the sheets laid around just about everywhere. Not only did the sheets make excellent roofs for our straw houses, but whenever we left some sheets long enough in the fields, we found nesting mice or grass snakes under them. They went straight to the Old Town's pet shop for the much-needed pennies.

The straw house was our little hiding place, away from our parents' prying eyes, where we could smoke some fags, pinched from home. You could say that we experimented too early.

One day, I, my brother and the rest of the Bembrook gang who remained, Steve, Phil, Mark, German, to name a few, aimed for a giant oak tree down in the bottom of the field. It was so huge that the branches looked like they reached the skies.

German Hatton was almost my brother's age, about fifteen, a well-built lad, with black hair and brown eyes. Attached to his head were a very large set of ears. His hair was cut old-fashioned, like a bowl had been put on his head. He was considered one of the bravest and toughest kids in our road, if not the toughest. It was a close call between him and my brother, Tony.

Edward was his birth name, but we called him, 'German.' Possibly, because he was crazy like a German or perhaps because he had a haircut like a German soldier.

Anyways, the magnificent German, our own Ted 'the marvelous' Hatton, had been to the boat yard where he got some rope and we decided that it would make a fantastic swing.

As I stared up into the gnarled branches of this huge tree, I realised this was going to be a daunting task.

German didn't think twice of climbing it though. He looped the rope round and round then flung it over his shoulder. After a big long stare upwards, and a deep breath, German began to scale what seemed like a mountain to climb. He climbed up and up until he found a suitable thick enough branch, the very one that stretched out over the field. German edged his way along the branch.

We were all holding our breath, while at the same time cheering him on, *"Go on Ted! You're nearly there."*

He reached the spot that had a clear fall for the rope to reach the ground.

German was as strong as an ox, because the rope must have weighed a ton. Yet he managed to tie it to that solid branch, then to drop the loose end down. He did it. Up went a cheer, and down came German climbing down the rope. He was the hero. We had no doubt we could rely on him to get things done.

That all sorted, we tied a good solid branch to the bottom of the rope for our seat. Then away we went, happy as Larry. The Oak Tree was up on the bank and the branch the rope was fastened to stretched out over the valley. So as the swing went out to its full length, we were probably 15 or 20 feet in the air. The norm was to jump on with the others as it was swinging to and fro with one of the other lads pushing us to make the swing go even higher. It could get a bit crowded and loud on the swing with a lot of shouting, laughing and 'hanging on for dear life'.

I wanted to join in the fun, so little me, all four or so stone of me (25 and a half kilos), jumped in with the big boys. Then as we sailed out to the swing's full length, I felt myself losing my grip on the return. I couldn't hold on any longer. I was snatched off by the force of gravity and down I fell, being knocked out as I hit the ground.

The next thing I knew, with my eyes still closed, I heard someone say, *"Is he dead?" "You'd better check his pockets,"* said someone else.

We were relatively poor kids in Bembrook road, so nothing went to waste.

"Better take his shoes too," said another.

Coming back to my senses, I exclaimed, *"Get me up!"*

I am not sure whether it was a sigh of relief or disappointment, but I was fine. The branches of the tree below had broken my fall, so I was just knocked out for a minute or two.

Getting hit like that was just a preview of what was soon to come.

Not far from our swing stood a massive white house, which had an even larger back garden with a swimming pool. There was also a giant green house that grew grapes, tomatoes, marrows and things like that inside. Birds used to fly in through the broken panes of glass. We would catch them and play with them for a while and then let them go. There were black birds, robins and sparrows, even bluetits, the most colourful of them all. The house used to belong to a well-known local man, Dr. Cutler, who was 'rumoured' to have vanished from a mysterious plane crash. Apparently, Dr Cutler went down in the English Channel, never to be seen again. Curious, we wanted to know if it was true. We thought we could ask if Mrs. Cutler needed anything to be done in the garden.

To our delight, we found out that the house was completely empty.

Immediately, we made the house our headquarters. It was a lot more spacious than our straw camp which we had built in the field. We even had a swimming pool and greenhouse with goodies to eat.

It was surreal, like in the movies.

The mystery man

One Saturday morning, when we arrived at the greenhouse to see if we could catch some birds, there was an old man sitting inside our greenhouse eating our grapes. He was quite tall and dressed rather shabby, with a trilby hat on. He had a short beard and a rucksack with pots and pans hanging from it as well as a sleeping bag.

"Hello, who are you?"

"I'm Sammy."

"I'm Paul. This is Steve, David and Alan," I said in return. And added, bravely,*" this is our camp."* He was smoking a roll up fag.

Sammy replied, *"I hope you don't mind, but I will be sleeping here for a while." "That's OK,"* we said. *"You can help us catch the birds."*

"I think its best if we let them out of the door," said Sammy. He explained, *"They get frightened when you catch them."*

"What's that you've got?" I asked.

"Oh, it's just my pens and pad," said Sammy. *"I like to draw things."*

He showed us his pad. There were nice drawings of birds and animals and a building with beams and lead glass windows. He told us stories of being a gunner in the army but that was all in the past. He preferred hopping from town-to-town, drawing and painting pictures of people, animals and houses to sell.

We liked Sammy. He was our secret friend. I never told Mum and our John about him. When Mum wasn't looking, I used to take some bread and cheese and one or two tins of stuff out from the cupboard, hide the goodies out in the yard and give them to Sammy. The other lads did it too. He was always very grateful.

To us, he was a good bloke who had lots of stories to tell. But then one day, he was gone. He disappeared as quickly as he came.

Sam opened my eyes to the reality of homelessness and that the 'wanderers' and 'homeless' have stories to share too, like you and me.

Fun at the movies and earning good and bad money

When I was about 9, I was employed by Harry, the Milkman. Harry used to pick me up at our house early in the mornings before I went to school. I would work only for an hour or so, but at the end of the week I would have a few shillings to spend at the pictures, called the ABC picture house located in Cambridge Road, down in Hastings Town Centre. Today it's called the ESK DIY store. My friends and I loved going to the picture house, especially when we all sung a song, "The ABC Minors," before the show began on Saturday mornings.

We would watch *The Three Stooges*, with Larry, Curly and Mo, and *Laurel and Hardy*. They were hilarious. We also saw some science fiction shows along with *Bugs Bunny, Micky Mouse, Donald Duck.* And then the ice cream lady would come round at the interval, adding to a fun packed Saturday morning. After the pictures, and if it were a sunny day, we would make our way down to the seafront.

We were very naughty boys and the seafront was our preferred destination.

Along the promenade, near the White Rock swimming baths, was a badminton size square pit where people would throw money for charity. After the people had gone, we would climb down into the pit, pick up their money, climb back out, and run.

Upon reaching Hastings Pier, we'd reach into our pockets, take out the cotton string we had brought with us and the sellotape, then we'd tape an old penny coin to the string of cotton. This was our preparation for the penny on a string trick. The Pier was a gold mine too you see. It was full of slot machines which we could fiddle the pennies from.

June and July were always good months of the year for earning some money. It was a strawberry season at Coghurst Lane strawberry farm. Usually myself, Steve, his brother, David and another Dave would meet up at the end of Bembrook for an hour Sunday morning stroll to the strawberry field.

We were no more than 10, but we sure knew our way around. We would often walk up to fifteen miles in three directions. North, East or West depending on what we had planned for that day; sea fishing, birds egging or looking for eels, crabs or fishes, which were left behind in the ebbing tide pools.

Once we noticed that no one seemed to be around in the farm, we would have a 'sort out' in the shed for some old crates, which held about twenty or thirty small punnets. Once our crates were full of strawberries, which took about an hour to pick, we would make our way back home.

I often wondered why no one ever chased us away. My theory is that whoever saw us, permitted the looting because we 'were only kids', after all.

I wished that it were not so. Remembering the incident at Mr. West's office, who, of course, only had good intentions in not punishing me for stealing from my Mum's purse, I now realised that tolerating even the slight misdemeanors of children could have serious consequences later on in life.

Any form of tolerance could harden the child's conscience. *"Spare the rod, and spoil the child,"* as Proverbs 13:24 in the Bible states.

Children may look innocent but they are capable of some wicked and strange things due to the deeper concept of the Original Sin, which we all have inherited from Adam and Eve as clearly told in the Bible.

Anyways, we sold our loot in the area. Most households loved strawberries in the summer for dessert. It wasn't a bad little earner.

I did not keep all my earnings to myself, but gave some to my Mum for some groceries for us.

Our birds' eggs hunting and the reckless tunnel expeditions

Between me and my brothers, Dean and Tony, I counted that we had collected almost 100 species of birds' eggs. In those days, bird egging was akin to butterfly catching or snake and lizard catching. It was not outlawed back then. It was merely a hobby, and, being kids, we didn't care much about the implications of what we did.

Most Saturdays, if I weren't working with Uncle Colin in his coal round or Harry the Milkman, we would go on our expeditions. Normally. we met at the end of Bembrook and whoever turned up that morning would be our gang for the day.

We always needed the bigger boys like German, Peter Coglan or Chris from upstairs with us, because they were good tree climbers. I liked having the bigger lads around us. It made me feel like I was a grown up too. Other lads in our neighbourhood, Steve, Dave and Roysten, would tag along with us sometimes.

Mostly, we liked going to Rye during spring time, which was from late March to May, and when the birds would be breeding and laying eggs.

Rye is a lovely little south east coastal town, about 13 or so miles from Hastings. It is one of the most beautiful towns in East Sussex, with its historic cinque port, cobbled streets, ancient Tudor houses and a beautiful, historic St. Mary's Church. Being in Rye, even for us kids, meant being transported into the past.

Upon arrival, we would pop into the bakers and spend some of our pocket money for some refreshments. You might wonder how we got our money? Well, both through resourcefulness and, again, shamefully stealing.

In Rye, we discovered some shallow ponds where eels lurked in the mud. It was not long before we caught them and sold them to Rye fish mongers. They took them all every time. We helped ourselves with the bus money too from the bus drivers' trays. While they stopped to have tea in the bus station, one of us would hop aboard and help ourselves. If the buses didn't have any change in them, then we'd find ourselves at the church on the top of the hill. Churches always have money boxes in them.

In the historic town of Rye.

Refreshed, we would then make our way to the rookery field along by the train gate crossing. The trees in the field where the Rooks nested were sycamore trees. Sycamore trees are awesome. They grow up to a 100-feet in height and can live up to 400 years.

When we weren't around, the Rooks' nests would be relatively safe from predators because they were so high on the Sycamore tree. There was only one among us all who was brave enough to attempt the task of climbing to the tops of these giant trees. And that was, again, 'The magnificent German', our own Ted 'the marvelous' Hatton!

By now the Rooks weren't at all happy with Ted, as he was about to scale the Everest of trees. The Rooks would circle defiantly around overhead, *'Kaah Kaahing,'* with bold resistance. To get to the first branch, Ted had to get up onto Pete's shoulders. Then slowly, with caution, Ted maneuvered his way up towards the top of the tree branches.

"Go on, Ted!" we encouraged.

Before long, Ted would be near the top, and that was the tricky part. Not only were the branches getting thinner, but the Rooks also dived bombed towards the oncoming predator, doing their best to protect their eggs.

On this day, Ted was not lucky. We heard, all of a sudden, an almighty crack of a branch snapping, followed by a loud *"ahhhhh!"*

We looked up as Ted came crashing down through the branches that, fortunately for Ted, were breaking his fall on his way down. Crack! Snap!*"Ahhh!"* Then, eventually, we heard a thud onto the soft grassy ground.

"Oh no!" We ran to Ted, but before we even got to him, he was back on his feet. *"Are you aright Ted*?" we screamed. Ted grunted his disapproval.

But he just brushed himself down, looked back up at the Rooks' nests and began his ascent once more. That was our Ted for you. Truly tough as iron and quite impressive really.

To get to our Rye destination, we would walk on a number of routes. Depending on the vote, maybe we would go along the coast under the Fairlight cliffs when the tide was out and where there would be an abundance of Herring gulls, Rock pigeons, Black backed gulls' eggs and so on. Or we would venture through Coghurst woods, where there would be Magpies' nests, Wood Pigeons, Blackbirds, Blue tits, Robins, Crows and on and on it went.

Or we would go the daring and most thrilling way of all, and that was through the mile-long tunnel. Looking back, we must have been either quite mad or fearless. We loved the thrill of going through the pitch-black train tunnel.

Let me describe how we did it.

At one particular time, the vote was to go through the Mile-long tunnel of Ore Village Station. To us kids, this tunnel was huge. Inside the tunnel, the lines were not electric, as the trains had diesel engines, which take them all the way to Ashford. But there was an electric third rail, located a few yards from the entrance of the Tunnel.

Soon I would find out how dangerous electric train line rails were.

"Are we ready?" one of the big boys would ask.

"*Yer, as ready as I'll ever be*", exclaimed the wee, little, snapper me.

Before we headed to the tunnel, either one or two of us would have to listen if any trains were coming. What we would do was to get down on our hands and knees, then put our ears onto the tracks to feel any vibrations, which meant an incoming train.

After getting the clear, *"Ok, let's go,"* we cautiously and closely moved in unison towards the tunnel.

The tunnel had a bend about half way through which we called the 'death bend'. Above the bend was a large round brick hole, which was a chimney. The chimney reached high and up until it reached out into a place called Coghurst Woods.

To this day, the chimney hole is still visible. That chimney hole was our landmark, which signaled that we were half way through, and from there we could see the light 'as small as it was', at the other end.

We rarely had a torch to use, so it wasn't long before we were in total darkness.

It was frightening. We could not even see our hands in front of our faces, and the older boys sometimes made scary noises.

We knew it was them, so it did not bother us. We would shout out our names and hear our voices echoing through the darkness.

Then, periodically, we'd stop to check to see if we were all still together, and have a listen, in case there was a rumble. The trains could come through every half hour. There would be at least one train which came through. Again, we relied on the vibrations to know which track and direction the train or trains were coming from.

If we did not hear any sounds, we carried on with our journey, very slowly. The only way we were able to get through the pitch black and not stumble over the track was to reach out with our hands onto the tunnel wall. The trick was to keep walking until we reached the death bend.

As soon as we heard, *"It's this side,"* we had to cross over the other track as fast as we could or stay on our side accordingly.

By then, it was every man for himself. The adrenaline that surged through my body was tremendous and that was one of the reasons why we did it.

I can remember on one occasion, that there were two trains that came through at the same time and one from each end. Now, that was tricky. We didn't know which way to turn, but we managed not to panic and to stay alive. We blindly ran until we came across a manhole, in time to crouch inside as the trains thundered past.

Getting to the chimney was 'a sigh of relief', because we could see some light. More importantly, it meant that we were near the end of the tunnel and at last we could say, *"There is light at the end of the tunnel."*

Indeed, our tunnel expeditions were extremely reckless, dangerous and even downright foolish, but it also brought interesting and fun memories.

One time, we found a cat in there with only 3 legs, so we decided to take it to a vet in Ore village.

Another time, when we got almost to the other end, there was a big cow standing in the entrance.

So, thinking very quickly, we started shouting, *"Go on, go on! Move, move, get out, you silly cow!"* while waving our arms around, shoving the animal out.

I ran up ahead and found a gate open and it wasn't long before we had her back in the field.

Everything said and done, and after a tiring day out, it was time to go home.

We never walked back home. We would ride the train, usually by walking back to Winchelsea Station, where we could take the train without paying. There was no ticket office or a station guard at the stop. After fifteen minutes or so the train alighted at the Ore Station, where there was no guard either.

And so, we were back home at last.

The lesson of a lifetime

As you very well know by now, the railway was a big part of our childhood adventures. We often played over the railway in the summer and even fed a huge pig kept there. The pig ate everything we gave him, including glass.

Sadly, the pig did not live long. In one of our visits, wondering if it was our fault for feeding him glass, we found it being pushed away dead on a barrow by its owner.

Our railway adventures not only brought fond memories but were also humbling, scary, and gave me one of the most memorable lessons in my life, 'Never play with live wires.'

It happened on a typical Saturday morning.

Through the hole in the fence, I, Steven and David went down the slope that led into the rails. Down by the tunnel entrance, there was the 'Third Rail', as we called it. One of the reasons we would go down there was because of the tadpoles which swam through a shallow brick well. We used to collect them and put them in our jam jars. There were even great Crested Newts there, too. Crested Newts are protected species nowadays.

Anyways, while we were there, playing around at the tunnel entrance, Steven must have been very savvy, because for some reason he jumped with both feet onto the third rail. He proudly claimed, "*You have to have one of your feet on the ground to get electrocuted.*"

How Steve knew that at 10 years old, I'll never know.

After a few seconds, Mr. Mischief came into action. I heard a whisper in my ear, "*Go and touch it. Don't worry, you won't get a shock and just think, you would look brave in front of your friends. You would be a hero!*"

Foolishly, I went over to the rail.

By this time, Steven and David were standing a few paces away.

"*Look!*" I said, and then as fast as lightning, I shot my hand out and touched the rail for a fraction of a second, pulling my hand straight back with no effect.

Mr. Mischief again whispered, "*Not like that. Hold onto it. It won't hurt you. Your friends would be so impressed.*"

I couldn't resist the temptation. I grabbed the live rail.

Nothing had ever, or has ever since, frightened me as much as what happened next. I'm writing this with shaking hands and tears in my eyes.

The shock that went through my whole body as a 9-year-old boy is difficult to put into words. It felt like I was being hit by a train. Somehow, all I could remember was being pulled quickly backwards, then lying on the railway sleepers.

I climbed to my feet and, without saying a word, I ran and I ran and I ran until I got home.

The front door was open, but Mum was in the kitchen.

I grabbed Mum and held onto her. *"What's the matter?"* she said. *"What's the matter*?" she repeated. *"Look at the state of you, you look like you have been hit by lightning."*

I could not say a word. I was alive! I didn't tell Mum about what happened to me that day, until many years later.

But out of curiosity back then, I found out that the live rail has 750 volts and 30.000 amps, which were needed to power a train.

God had His hands on me that day.

When I was 20 and weighing in for a professional boxing fight at the Royal Albert Hall, I found the courage to tell Mum what happened.

I said, *"Mum, I want to tell you something. Do you remember the time when I was a kid and I came home looking like I'd seen a ghost and just couldn't speak?"*

"Yerrrr", said Mum.

"Well, I'd been down to the railway and got electrocuted. I grabbed the live rail."

"What!?" she screamed.

I quickly got out of the way, before she could give me a good hiding. To her, I remained her little boy.

I won my fight for Mum that night.

With Henry Cooper after one of my fights.

CHAPTER 8

Discovering Boxing and The West Hill Boxing Club

Boxing

At five, I had developed a keen interest in boxing.

At that early age, I remember that I used to watch boxing on television. I watched Cassius Clay, or 'the great Muhammad Ali', as he later became known as. I watched him fight our very own Henry Cooper in May 1966. Back then, every time there was boxing on television, I would watch while shadow boxing around the front room, usually with my big brother, Tony.

Later on, I would personally meet Henry Cooper in one of my fights. The first time he came to see me, he went to my dressing room, wished me well and told me to, *"Keep your hands, up son."* I once held his Lonsdale belt and loved the feel of it, saying to myself, *"I want one of these."*

I liked Henry. It was a pity that in his fights he'd cut so easily. One of Henry's memorable fights was when he fought Ali for the first time at Wembley Stadium in June 1963 in front of a 35.000 crowd. Henry gave a lot of weight away leading up to that fight. He was twenty pounds lighter than Clay. It was touch and go for the first 4 rounds, with Clay fooling around, jabbing, moving, and picking Henry off. But then Henry backed Clay to the ropes and unleashed 'Enry's Ammer', his numbing left hook, catching Clay square on the jaw. What a shot, that was! Like a lumberjack shouting, *"Timber!"* Clay came down like a man losing his legs. Clay was rescued by the bell. Not only that, but mysteriously, Angelo Dundee, Clay's trainer, called the referee over and pointed at Clay's right glove, which was thirty seconds into rest time. It had somehow split open. *Ummm!* So, a new pair was fetched to glove up Clay before the fight could continue, which gave him more than enough time to recover. Clay went on to cut Henry to pieces in 2 minutes, 15 seconds into the fifth round. Referee Tommy Little had no other choice but to stop the fight. It was all over bar the shouting.

Back to our story. I was 9 years old when I started learning the fundamentals of boxing. I had heard through the Bembrook Road grapevine, that there was a boxing club down at the bottom of Whitefriars Road, not too far from where we lived. David Mepham, who lived not too far along the road from us, told me that it was called the 'West Hill Boys Club' and that he'd been down there a couple of times. So, I asked Mum if it was OK to go with David. Anyways, subs was a shilling and it was only once or twice a week.

Mum agreed, and added that it would do me the world of good to have a bit of discipline. Not too sure, about the discipline part, but I was very curious about the club.

So, the next day I asked David if he was going to the club next Thursday.

We arranged that I would knock for him at 6.30pm on the next coming Thursday evening. He asked me to wear an old pair of track bottoms and a pair of plimsolls. That Thursday never came, though, because David, his brother Steven and I were brought home by a policeman in their panda car. We had been up at Rock Lane Farm House. The owner, Farmer Eldridge caught us in his hay barn, which we had completely wrecked. We were making straw bale camps and we kicked them all over the place. Farmer Eldridge took us to his house to teach us a lesson. He rang the police.

They came and took us home. My backside was sore from our John's size 9 slippers that day.

Yes, I was also disciplined growing up. My parents never tolerated my misdemeanors. But there are things beyond your parents' control. More than half the time, and for obvious reasons, I never told Mum and John what we did out in the fields, in the railway, or in school.

The next Thursday, my Mum gave me a shilling with pleasure, just to get me into something worthwhile, and with the parting words, *"You make sure you get there and behave yourself!"*

And so, it was time to knock for David. One of David's sisters, Julie or Jackie, would normally open the door. They were a year or two older than me and were always smiling. Out came David, looking sharp and ready for a round or two.

Off we went. I was so excited to find how the evening would unfold.

On arrival, Mr. Phillpotts was the first man I noticed. He looked more like a Chicago gangster than the club secretary. He was a very smart man with a rugged face that had a big round red nose on it. Mr. Phillpotts always wore a trilby hat, a trench coat, and pinstriped trousers with bright shiny brogue leather shoes. He collected the subs, which I soon learned to dodge so I could, instead, buy a bag of chips from next door at the Whitefriars Chippy.

Back then, the club was a two-story building which closely resembled a structure which had been hit by a German Luftwaffe air raid. But understandably, as those times were hard and money was short. There were no shower facilities. The changing room shower facilities only had a bucket, with cold running water. The walls looked scorched in places and the green and white paint, which were the club's colours, were peeling off from the damp walls. The floor was old wooden boarding and badly fitted. The boxing gym on the floor above didn't look much better either.

But at least it had a ring, some big mirrors, bags, speed balls and weights. It also had big square horse hair mats and benches. The heating consisted of a couple of old electric bar heaters which we used to warm ourselves with in the winter. That is if, or when, we had time to stand around the gym. If we didn't keep moving, we may well have had a technical knock-out by Jack Frost.

All in all, it was a rough and ready boxing gym that through the years would produce some fine boxing champions. West Hill Boxing Club remains to this day a boxing club but has kept up with the times.

Later on, with my mate John in one of the school championships fights.

And so, I walked in the gym, all ready to go, wearing my old tracky bottoms with plimy's to match. All 4st something and 4ft nothing of me was about to do some proper boxing. If you could only see me then, with my sweet little freckles and bright blonde hair. You wouldn't have thought that butter would melt in my mouth, so Nanny Edith used to tell me.

David introduced me to his trainer, Jim Hart. I also met Brian and Eddy, the latter was our Sunday school teacher, and Jack.

Jim didn't say much to me at first. He just asked my name, ruffled my hair and said "Good lad." So I went and stood by the wall to watch as the other kids were doing their thing. There were about 20 or so young boys there. They were punching bags, skipping, shadow boxing in the mirror, doing sit ups, press ups and listening to the trainers calling out numbers while punching pad gloves, which were on the trainers' hands.

Close by, there was a pile of old horse hair gloves and pad mittens.

"Let's put a pair of these on," I thought. *"I'd seen plenty of boxing on the telly, so let's try it out."*

The mittens, both right and left hands, were the smallest I found from the pile on the table, but they fit me perfectly. They didn't smell too good though. There was a bag that was hanging free. It was a big brown leather bag that hung from one of the metal girders above. The old bag was patched up a bit, here and there, just like the rest of the gym. I tested it out with a left-right, left-right combination, which I had seen the pros doing on the television. It was a soft bag, which suited me because I would find out later that some of the bags were as hard as rock.

Finding out it was a soft bag, I went into action, just like what I did with my brother, Tony, back home. Being an attention seeker, I am fond of showing off. One of my many inherent flaws, I suppose. So I skipped around the bag throwing jabs and left – right combinations, trying to copy what I'd seen our Henry, Clay and the others do on the telly.

It wasn't long before I could see from the corner of my eye that I was being watched by Jim and Brian, the trainers and the other lads.

The bell that was up on the wall rang out a welcome clang. I stopped to have a rest. It seemed like the right thing to do.

Jim asked where I'd been boxing before I came to the West Hill. He was surprised to find out that I'd never been to a boxing club before and that I was only doing what I had seen on TV. Jim said I was a 'natural.'

And so, there was a lot of excitement during my first night at the West Hill Boys Club. It immediately dawned on me that this is the place where I wanted to be. I especially loved the attention that I got.

From then on, the West Hill Boys Club became my newly found adopted family, and of course became a huge part of my life, specifically throughout my teenaged years.

Our West Hill B.C. produced a formidable group of both junior and senior boxers always prepared for any event. Just to name a few, there were: Gary Gates, Gary Smith, Gary's brother Kim Smith, George Dollen, Paul Joy, Fred Frewin, Mick O'Mara, Paul Allen, Dave Bishop, Andy Pendleton, Mick Richford, Brian Collins, Joey Ellis, Ian Gray and many others.

During our time, we fought the best of the best and went up against other boxing clubs up and down the length and breadth of the country.

In one of our boxing competitions, with fellow West Hill Boxing Club boxers: Kim Smith, George Dollen, Joey Ellis, and Mick O' Mara.

The entire town of Hastings supported us and it was always a sight to see when we would set off in our little Commer diesel mini-bus, ready and willing to box anyone, anywhere, anytime.

Our green and white club kits were always kept immaculately clean and pressed. The unsung heroines, Joan Fitchett, her daughter, Vicky and our well-loved supporters never let us down.

We had a lot of fun combined with tears of joy and sorrow from some of our losses but it would be the most unforgettable first 9 years of my boxing career at the West Hill Boxing Club.

First boxing competitions and my teenaged years

At 10 years old, I was given the clearance by the appointed doctors to take part in boxing competitions. Because of my natural abilities in the gentlemanly art of pugilism, I was transferred from the Junior section of the West Hill to the Seniors in a matter of only a few weeks. I was the youngest Junior ever to join the Seniors at such a young age.

I won most of my fights. The only time I didn't win a fight was when I'd been sniffing too much petrol, dropping LSD tabs or smoking far too much cannabis. Yes, as you will find out, on the coming pages, I discovered drugs at an early age of 13.

Aged 13, with some of my trophies.

Unfortunately, boxing did not give me the discipline and restraint to keep me from troubles, as my Mum had hoped for.

When I turned 11, I was taken to the police station for stealing a Swiss army knife from a local fishing tackle shop. I received a caution and, of course, a few lashes from our John, using his 'infamous slippers'.

Getting a caution was the norm for us boys, mainly because we were too young to be taken to court for minor criminal offenses. To me, that was a green light to continue what I did. Knowing that I could easily get away with it made me indifferent. In fact, I just made sure that I was not caught the next time Mr. Mischief told me to steal.

At 12, I started going to the Priory Road Secondary School Annex located at Dudley Road. We had to spend a school year there before we went to the Seniors up at the Priory.

At the same time, Mum and our John found a new council house place to live at Brendon Rise, Broomgrove Estate. It had an extra bedroom and Mum said we should take it because it would keep us brothers, me, Tony and Dean, away from fighting and all the 'riff-raff' over in our former place at Bembrook Road.

Soon over at Broomgrove, Tin Town, I was making new friends. My new school, at Dudley Annex, was not far away from our new house either. It took 20 minutes to walk to school through short cuts.

Dudley Annex was a fascinating building with steep sloped pointed roof tops on top of the lower middle and upper floor class rooms. Situated on the third floor was the Assembly Hall, where we enjoyed our Physical Education classes with Mr. Marshal. But better still, on Fridays, just before home time for the weekend, Mr. James, our Headmaster would give us all a few numbers from his piano recital culminating with 'The John B Sails', sung by the Beach Boys. A great sing-a-long song which always sent us all home in high spirits. Mr. James always enjoyed his Friday one-man concert shows just as much as we did.

Unexpected brushes with death, once again

In the summer, after our mid-week field sports day at Priory Road, which we held at the East Hill and which I truly enjoyed the most in school, I and my friends, Craig Marsh, Gideon Peters, Iven, John and Mark Baker, hunted for Gulls' eggs and adder snakes. The poisonous adder snakes easily fetched us 20 shillings or so down at the Old Town Pet Shop.

From the East Hill, we hurried over to the cliff tops of Fairlight Glen. The beaches and rocks below were over a 125 feet shear drop to the rocky bottom, 'a tidy fall'. We had no fear, and risking our lives seemed fine, also for the prize of a rare Black Backed Gull's egg.

"*There's one,*" said Mark excitedly.

"*Let me go,*" I replied.

I was the smallest and could climb down faster. I got near to the very edge, when suddenly, the loose earth beneath me gave way and I thought this was it, a slide toward my final breath here on earth. I shouted, "*Mark! Mark! Throw me your satchel strap.*"

Like a thunder bolt, Mark leaped into action. Just before I went over the edge to my certain death, I managed to grab the life line. Mark held it tightly then hauled me back to safety.

From that day on, heights gave me the creeps. Nowadays, I avoid heights as much as possible, even my belly churns at the mere thought of it.

On our way back home, as I was telling the lads with great relief that it was good to be alive from such a close call, we spotted an adder snake, basking in the late afternoon sun. The adder is the only venomous snake native to Britain, which is easily recognizable by the zigzagging black and brown markings, which go down from head to tail.

Being recklessly cocky, I bragged, "*Let me catch it. Look, I'll show you how to do it.*"

I grabbed our 20 shillings by the tail. *"Gotcha!!"* I said with glee.

But a snake is an inherently treacherous reptile. With one swift curl maneuvering, it found its way to my thumb and bit me. Blood dripped over my thumb and I started sucking on the wound, like crazy while the others had a good laugh.

When I got home, I showed my little wound, that had swollen a wee bit, to Mum. I said I felt a bit dizzy, and I played sick for a whole week.

The story going around school was that I was dying from snake poisoning.

In reality, I was enjoying the time of my life at home, skiving off, with my feet up and pleading, *"Please Mum, Mum, can I have...?"*

Experimenting with drugs and breaking the law

As I grew older into my teenaged years, I was schooled at Priory Road Seniors, and still behaving like the school clown, not learning much at all. But being street wise, I thought I knew it all.

At 13, I became more daring and bolder than ever. I and my friends experimented with illicit drugs. We smoked cannabis, sniffed solvents, took LSD and speed.

The drugs started with cannabis. During the summer at school, most days on our lunch time break, we went down to our classmate, Gideon's house.

He'd go and retrieve the solid brown substance from the most obscure of places. Then we'd all watch what he would do next. My blood would be pumping excitedly around my veins as Gideon rolled up a joint. When rolled, we'd go out into the garden and disappear to the very back and hide behind the bushes. After lighting it up, it was passed around. We would deeply inhale the smoke and exhaled towards the hovering flies and insects, then laughed when they dropped from the sky. We'd smoke just one joint between us, and that was quite enough. Then we'd make our way back to our school's afternoon classes; mainly talking gibberish and laughing our heads off at just about everything and nothing.

One time, I was in Mr. Catt's class for my daily afternoon English language lessons when the high had worn off. I could hardly open my eyes and would slump my head on the desk. *"Wake up, Huggins!"* Mr. Catt would shout. *"I'm not very well, Sir,"* usually came the reply.

On other days, we went down Whitefriars Hill, opposite the school, to the shop at the bottom of the hill. Arnolds pop in was a good place for buying cigarettes and lighter fuel. We'd then go over to the West Hill, where there was a mass of dense Ivy plants, which we could bounce on like a trampoline. We'd smoke the fags and sniff the petrol to get a hallucinogenic high. Then we would go back to school as sick as pigs, hardly able to stand up.

Our criminal activities also worsened and became rampant.

I mean, by the time I was almost 14 years old, the club secretary, Jimmy Mac, my trainer Johnny Gray and other club officials along with my Mum, had already accompanied me on my appearances to the Juvenile Court, not only once but on numerous occasions. I'd been convicted of car theft, shop lifting, burglary and on it went. I was only saved from being taken away to an approved school on numerous occasions because of the immaculate references from the West Hill Boys Boxing Club. Otherwise, I would have been thrown away and locked up, repeatedly.

You can imagine that my DBS is several pages long, detailing all my criminal activities. Of course, I am totally ashamed of it all. My criminal record also kept me from employment opportunities at times. Understandably so!

Training with Johnny Gray for the National School Boy Championships.

On reflection, Mr. Mischief had grown to Mr. Destroyer. Such is the way of the evil one. It is a destroyer. It pursues you. It takes hold of your entire being into many ways you cannot control. It overpowers your conscience to the point of no return. To a point where no one could ever save you, except, as you will learn later on, Jesus. Today, I can plainly see why the world is the way it is. The Devil is the Prince of this world, as even the Bible says he is so.

Let me be clear though, that while Mr. Mischief, which I now call Mr. Destroyer, was, you could say, the main culprit, I was very much a willing participant to his devious, repeated schemes. As I will explain later, we are not here on earth by mere chance. God created us. It is also not a mystery that God created us, not as robots, but He gave us free will to choose and to act accordingly.

I can hardly believe that I am able to tell you this story and there is so much more to come, even of near-death experiences. You could say it took me a very long time to learn my lesson. The saying, 'a cat has nine lives' might very well apply to me, but I am alive, as you are, for a purpose.

CHAPTER 9

My love for Kentucky Fried Chicken and the year 1975

At 14 years old I'd won 32 out of my 34 fights. Because of my size, I boxed at the lowest weight level. I was even lower than the lowest weight stipulation for the British School Boys' Championships.

This year, 1975, we were going for gold.

My trainers Johnny Gray and Dave Harris had developed a special weight to tip me into the lowest weight class. We called our secret weapon, 'Jeffery'. Jeffery was a triangular piece of lead roof flashing molded to fit into my crutch.

This year we had a code. Just before the weigh-in for one of our championship fights, we talked in the weigh-in room and in the presence of the officials.

Dave or John would say, *"Have you seen, Jeffery?"* I would reply. *"Yes, he got on the bus and went home."* That was the code that Jeffery was now safely in place. Jeffery weighed about 10 ounces, just enough so that I would tip the scales, even before I got on the scale. Dave or John would get me to drink as much water or milk as I could get inside of me. I had so much milk in me one time that just after tipping inside the weight limit and getting back off the scales, I couldn't hold it all in any longer. It all came rushing out over everybody. The officials knew what I'd been up to but they let it go. They knew I was good enough to beat anyone, even if I had to 'ridiculously add to my weight'.

The year before, we thought my opponent, Gary Kettle,

would not turn up and so we mistakenly let our guard down. One of the lads' Dad, Pat O'Mara, went and bought a large bucket of Kentucky fried chicken to celebrate. I almost ate the lot.

Unfortunately, to my dismay, Gary turned up. He ended up beating me on a majority decision, two rounds in three. Chicken wasn't my favorite bird that day. Gary was one of the very few boys who had ever beaten me.

This year, though, I had taken Gary out in the Southern

One fight from a national title

Hungry Huggins out to destroy Smart boy

By Paul Woolwich

There is an old saying in the fight game that the only good boxer is a hungry one, and West Hill's young Paul Huggins, who tonight makes his bid for a title in the National Schoolboy Championships at Blackpool, is such a boxer.

Pint-sized Paul has an insatiable appetite for the sport and for food and it was the latter that caused his downfall in last year's championships when he looked set to storm his way to the top.

At Brighton in the first round of the competition, Huggins met Crawley's Freddie Lyons. The result should have been academic, the West Hill boy should have walked away with it.

But moments before he was due to step into the ring Huggins devoured a whole bucketful of Kentucky Fried Chicken and awkward, went out on a majority decision much to the delight of Lyons.

It was a stupid mistake that is unlikely to be repeated and remains the only blot on the young boxer's copy-book.

The only person who stands between Huggins and the All-England title is K. Sanasi, a rugged little Welsh champion.

Smart won his way through to the Blackpool final the hard way by defeating the reigning NBB champion. K. Wallace, of the Golden Gloves Club, Liverpool, in the semi-finals on a majority decision.

It was not the result that the Hastings club wanted or, indeed, expected, and they would have preferred to have had their boy up against Wallace. Smart is

Huggins' trainer, Johnnie Gray, is not unduly worried and feels that on his present form the Priory Road schoolboy will win the title and with it the possibility of securing for himself a place in the England team.

Thirteen - year - old Huggins has been boxing for the past three years. He is short and thin with a mop of unruly blonde hair. To date he has had 19 fights, of which he has won all but three, and most of those have been against top class opposition.

He seems to thrive on destroying boxers with reputations and his slight frame disguises a deceptively strong punch which he complements with neat footwork and amazing stamina.

Once in the ring he is highly adaptable and has the all-round ability to cope with any situation. He can stand and box or alternatively he can stand and 'just swop punches, but he is a boxer first and a street fighter second.

He will not be without support tonight as 50 people are making the trip to the North West seaside resort and a coach party from the

Route to the final

Young Paul Huggins steps into a Blackpool ring tonight (Saturday) in an attempt to become only the second Sussex boxer to win a National Schoolboy Championship since 1963. This is how he got there:—

January 31: In the Sussex finals held at Brighton, Huggins defeated P. Millis, of Moulsecomb, over three rounds with a unanimous decision and he took the county title.

finalist.

February 8: In the regional finals staged at Aldershot, Huggins destroyed K. MacMillan, of Basingstoke, again on a unanimous decision.

four with a convincing win over S. Rodgers, of Northamptonshire, on a unanimous decision.

March 3: He won his ticket to the Blackpool finals for again

Newspaper clipping from the Observer of The KFC ARTICLE.

Counties' Finals. It was a long hard climb to get to the finals in the British School Boys' Championships.

There weren't too many Hastings boys then in the 34 years of

Hastings boxing history who had ever reached the finals. Some of those were Joey Lee, Fred Frewin and Dave Bishop. 1975 was my year.

It was not a walk in the park to get to the finals, but I was determined from the onset. If I can remember correctly, the first round of the championships were the preliminaries, and that included the local clubs in Hastings and further out around the South East. If you won those, then came the Southern Counties, and if you won those, it stretched up into the Midlands and again, if you won against the Midlands, you had to fight against all the other Counties, and then came the quarter finals, the semis and finally, the finals. The Grand Finals would of course, decide who the British Schoolboy Champion would be.

I was down to fight Kelvin Smart from Wales. Kelvin was a tough young lad, and to me he looked like the 'Incredible Hulk'! I wasn't mature for my age and still without a single hair yet on any part of my body except for my head of course. And I could see at the weigh-in that Kelvin had big muscles and hairy legs. I had a feeling he was going to be more powerful than me.

There were lots of people who came from Hastings to see the fight and to support me.

The pressure was almost too much to bear. My brother, Tony, was there with his friend, the great late singer song-writer John Martyn. John was an amazing musician who had played alongside Eric Clapton.

If you have ever been nervous just before you were going to do something brave and exciting or take a driving test, that is how I felt every time I climbed into the boxing ring. But as soon as the bell went, I focused. Focusing relieved my fears. I would measure up my opponent, then strike like a cobra.

Only this time, the nerves were 10 times more intense, and it was terrifying.

All was set and we made our way to the ring.

Kelvin was already in the ring, warming up. My trainers were telling me things that I could barely hear. My heart was pounding as I stepped up into the arena. The Master of Ceremonies announced our names and our schools. Huge shouts of encouragement came from the crowd.

Gum shield in, the first-round bell sounded. I could only do one thing and that was to fight for my life and for our West Hill Club's reputation and for Hastings. They had been so good to me. If nothing else, I wanted to win this for them as much as it was for me.

Finally, after what seemed like a lifetime, the fight began. The first round went well, if not with caution. I landed some good punches and I spent much of the time on my front left foot, because I'm right-handed and an 'orthodox boxer'. It means I stand with my left foot in the front and right at the back, with my right hand at the back, ready to throw the hard punches at long ranges. So I flicked out left jabs and the right left right combinations, followed by numbing body shots. Kelvin was exchanging as good as he took, and at last the first bell rang to end the first round.

Back in my corner, John talked me through on what we should be doing. I nodded my head in agreement, and did my best to listen, but never really understood a word John or Dave were saying. They could have been from another planet, speaking another language.

Kelvin was a strong boy who hit me hard, but he didn't have my speed. I piled the pressure on until the end was near. All I could hear in the dimly lit background were voices shouting out, "*Forward! Paul! Forward! Slip the shots! Use the left right left right…*"

Of course, the crowd meant well, but you just do your own thing in boxing.

At last, the final bell rang for the end of the third round. I went back to the corner. John and Dave said it can go either way, but what a cracking match it had been. We were called into the centre of the ring. We were congratulated for such a superb performance and that it was sad that there had to be a loser.

The result was announced and resounded around the great hall. *"The winner is, by a majority decision, the blue corner from Hastings Priory Road School, Paul Huggins!"*

And that was me.

I could not believe it. The hall went crazy with euphoria and

PAUL HUGGINS — NATIONAL SCHOOLBOY BOXING CHAMPION

This has been a very successful year for Paul Huggins of 4E. In January 1975 Paul defeated schoolboy McNillan to become champion of Sussex. A member of West Hill Boys' Club, Paul went on to represent Sussex against Surrey, fighting Gary Kettle. He then went on to the Regional Championship where he met and defeated Macmillan.

After swift success in both the quarter and semi-finals Paul set off for Blackpool to make his challenge for the championship. Matched against the strong Welsh schoolboy Kelvin Smart, Paul knew that he was in for a difficult fight. Although some supporters had accompanied Paul for the event, there was overwhelming support for his opponent. During the fight Smart was reprimanded by the referee for repeated butting. Paul, boxing with great skill, won the bout on a narrow points margin.

He received a handsome trophy for his success and is entering the championship competition again this year. He can be sure of the support and good wishes of all members of the school.

of course, disappointment from the Welsh fans. We had done it! It was a fantastic achievement, by all concerned and all the hard work and preparations paid off.

The trouble with me though, was this: I would burn the candle at both ends and rely almost entirely on my natural born abilities. My stamina would beat me.

Having a good stamina in any sports is crucial. A super fit man who's not so talented could beat a talented man who is not super fit. You must develop and have a good stamina to be a true champion.

I would learn this lesson the hard way.

CHAPTER 10

The crash landing

There was nothing quite like the euphoric high than performing and winning in a major event like what I had just managed to achieve.

Big credits to those concerned who had so far kept me out from being incarcerated in some sort of disciplinary institution.

But that was all about to change. No sooner from being the British schoolboy boxing champion, flying as high as a kite, to the very next morning after we had got back from Blackpool.

There was a knock on our front door. Mum opened it and there standing on the front door to my disappointment and fearful dismay, 'but not really surprised', were a plain clothed police officer and a lady Probation Officer.

I was told to pack a bag. The Probation Officer was taking me to Redhill Approved School.

No! My great achievement bubble burst right there and then. Down I came, crashing from a great height into a pile of nothingness, all in shattered pieces and gone, caput. It seemed like my world was crushed, and now I had to pay, and rightly so, for my crimes of car theft and other unruly behavior, which my dear and kind Mum couldn't bear to handle anymore.

A little case was packed with underwear and other garments. I was soon to find out that I wouldn't be needing those. This institution had prison rules and their own clothes for me to wear, like it or not. With tears, I said good bye to Mum. I was about to go on a journey to where a little lad like me was going to face some harsh realities within the penal correctional reform school.

I was escorted to sit in the back of a plain red Morris car, and while the Probation Officer and I were waiting to leave, the police man spoke with my Mum. Then they took me away with them.

The journey to Redhill, Surrey took what seemed like a lifetime. Not a word was spoken. We eventually reached the institution's gates. This was the very same castle gates that I'd come to 9 or so years back to visit my brother, Tony.

The gates were opened and we went inside. I was taken to a dismal plain white painted room with wooden chairs and a plain oak wood desk. I was told to sit down. The Probation Officer discussed the formalities.

Then they told me to return to the car. We drove down past some high fences with barbed wire curling around the tops, past a field where there were a hundred or so inmates shouting and doing military drills.

Finally, we reached a large, outhouse building. From there, I was taken into a reception area and booked into my new place of residence for the next 6 weeks. I never got to see the lady Probation Officer again.

Six weeks of sorrow at Redhill

"Huggins!" said the smartly dressed officer.

"What?" I answered.

*"Don't what me lad. I'm, Mr. Shaw or Sir to you, boy. I'm your administration officer! You're not at home now, lad. And stand up straight while I'm talking to you little man. Do you understand?
"said Mr. Shaw* sternly.

"Yes, sir!" I said, trying to keep my wits about me. *"What is this place?"* I thought to myself.

I was taken to a shower room. Told to strip and shower then told to go through a foot bath. I was then sent to the clothing, toiletries and utensils department.

There, I was given the smallest pairs of gray trousers and jeans that could be found, along with a blue and white striped shirt and an additional light grey shirt. They also handed me a towel, a tooth brush, some soap, shoes, and gym pumps. Then I was handed a plastic cup, a plate, a bowl, all with a plastic knife, spoon and fork.

Next, I was taken to a dormitory with 30 or so beds in it. I was shown to my bed, which had an upright brown cabinet besides it and that was where I would keep my bits and pieces.

I was then taken along a corridor to another room and told that I must do an IQ test. Believe it or not, my IQ turned out to be just above average. After the test, I returned to the dormitory and told to wait until the other boys got back from their exercise drill. Only then, we would go down for our late afternoon tea.

With final instructions from Mr. Shaw, who said that I would soon learn what to do by watching and following the others. "*Look after your things, keep your head down, your mouth shut, and do as you're told by the Officers, then you'll be OK. If not, you will have to learn the hard way,*" reminded Mr. Shaw.

"*What could be harder than this?*" I thought. I certainly was in no hurry to find out what the hard way was, that's for sure.

I looked at the clock on the wall and wondered if it actually worked. It seemed it didn't want to tick at all, but yes it did work. It went slowly round until it reached 4.30pm, just after that the boys began to filter into our dormitory.

Nobody took much notice of me at first, but then one of the bigger boys came and asked my name and what I'd done to be in there.

"*I'm Paul Huggins,*" I said, hoping that he might have heard of me. There was no response, so I continued with my crimes, hoping to get a reaction, "*Oh, I did nothing impressive, just stealing cars and robbing shops, like everybody else.*"

His name was Arthur and he was about 15 or 16. Arthur finally responded, "*We go down for tea at five o'clock, just follow me.*"

He then walked over to his bed to get ready. Arthur was a half cast lad with a big Afro hairstyle. He looked like he kept himself in good condition, with muscles everywhere. It was good to be spoken to by someone. I liked Arthur straight away.

The bell rang. It was the teatime bell. Everyone began walking to the kitchen hall in an orderly fashion, which was down the stairs and across the yard. As instructed, I followed Arthur. The boys were coming from other dormitories, too. I watched the other boys with interest. They each picked up a dinner tray and so I followed suit. Then we queued up to where we collected our food.

On getting to the hatch, I was delighted to see John. He was someone I knew from Priory Road School. John was a kitchen orderly. Apparently, the best jobs to have were to work in the kitchens, for obvious reasons. Sometimes when I was ordered to clean the parade yard, I would sneak in and have a quick chat with John where he'd give me a cup of sweet milky tea, a rare treat in prison. I was sad when it was John's time to leave. He'd served his time, and I'd lost a friend. But hey, he was free at last.

Being away from home and being in Redhill institution was tough. I got on as best with everybody as I could, and did 'within reason,' what I was told to do by the Officers.

Word got through to me that I had been chosen to box for England against Wales. So I was given permission by the Governor to go for early morning runs around the grounds and out into the fields. I could have run away if I had wanted to. I thought about it, but what would be the point? I would only get caught again and would have to do a longer sentence, getting even more punishment.

Besides all that, I was only serving six weeks. The authorities told me, *"If you don't pull your socks up and start behaving yourself, this is what you can expect more of in the future."*

My 6 weeks soon came round, even though it seemed that the clocks never went fast enough. I hadn't learned much in Redhill, except that detention robbed me of my friends, my boxing and my family. I missed my Mum, our John and my brothers.

It was, at last, my time to leave. I swore I would never be back. At least not to that place I wouldn't.

As for the fight, I was training to fight for, well, it turned into a capital D, spelt Disaster.

Shortly after my release from Redhill, we made our way down to Swansea across the Welsh border. Coming from prison, I wasn't in the best of mental health. On top of all that, I felt the worse for wear from travel sickness.

When we eventually got there for the weigh in, it turned out that I was 10 pounds, underweight. I wasn't at all keen to give the weight away. I felt bad and upset.

I decided I didn't want to fight.

Considering the past few weeks, I spent in Redhill and all, I think I lost my nerve. Realizing, as well, that I was human after all.

Back to town and at Priory

Back home, I was treated by the public as the new sports star around town. I enjoyed the headlines in the local press that said, "National Title for Huggins" and "Huggins Joins Town's National Heroes". I was being hailed as a hero at school. Mr. Kimber, our Priory Road School headmaster announced my name in the school assembly. He said I was the only Priory Road Schoolboy to have ever achieved what I have done. Mr. Kimber said that the school was very proud of me.

Nevertheless, as a Priory Road student, as you could tell from the previous Chapters, I must have been one of the worst ever. My behaviour in class was more than appalling. All I wanted to do was play the fool and drive the teachers mad. They told me, time and again, to stand outside the class room until I was called back in. Surely, I did not make it easy for them.

I was so insensitive and such a pain that, one time, I was told to go to Mr. Broughton's class. You couldn't mess around with

Mr. Broughton. He was very strict. He was highly and fearfully respected for his ability to flip his lid and cane you for the least of offenses. Mr. Broughton turned to write some Maths on the black board. For me, it was an ideal opportunity to launch my water bomb that I had prepared earlier. That was suicide but splat it went. It landed just above Mr. Boughton's head. Covering him with water. The class erupted in laughter. Mr. Broughton was a tall slim man, who had a hairstyle similar to Adolf Hitler.

Our old school: Priory Road.

Humiliated, he reached for the cane on his desk top and slammed it down on to the books. *"WHO DID THAT?!"* he shouted. The class fell silent. You could have heard a pin drop. *"WELL?"* he asked again. Nobody uttered a word.

"Right!" he warned, *"You're all staying behind after school. You will all write a thousand lines! Do you hear me? Who was it?"* repeated Mr. Broughton.

Not wanting to keep the class back at school, I decided to do the right thing. I put my hand up. *"Sorry, Sir, it was me,"* I admitted, almost bursting into laughter.

"*I should have guessed,*" Mr. Broughton said.

"*Get out here Huggins, I'm going to give you something to laugh about sonny boy!*"

I walked out to the front of the 30 something students' class. "*Bend over,*" said Mr. Broughton bending his cane, almost touching end to end.

"*No, sir,*" I said.

"*What did you say, Huggins? BEND OVER LAD!*"

"*No, Sir, I'm not letting you cane me, Sir. Only my Headmaster, Mr. Kimber can cane me, Sir,*" I insisted, stubbornly.

It took him a second or two to answer, but then he exploded. "*Right!! Come, with me, Huggins,*" and off we marched to the Headmaster's office.

Inside the office, Mr. Broughton explained what I had done and how insolent I had been. "*OK, Mr. Broughton, thanks for telling me. I'll deal with this. You'd better get back to your class.*"

With that, Mr. Broughton went out and shut the door behind him.

I recognised Mr. Kimber. He always wore a sports jacket with a nice pair of baggy cords. He was a smart man with a kind heart.

Mr. Kimber gave me a good talking to and explained that I could do so much better at school, and that I had a lot going for me.

"*It is such a terrible waste, young man. But under the circumstances, I'm sorry, but I'm going to have to cane you, Paul.*"

"*OK, Mr. Kimber,*" quite moved as I bent over to touch my toes.

Mr. Kimber got his cane, and then very lightly tapped me on the backside.

"*Run along lad, and let's have some more effort in class please, and don't forget to shut the door.*

"*Thank you, Sir,*" I exclaimed, and hurried down the corridor.

Just like that, and again not sure if it really did me good, but I escaped punishment, twice from a School Headmaster.

An overdose

In another instance that I felt unwell, my Mum called up our Priory Road Surgery Doctor. Dr. Daz was an Indian man, who gave Mum just about anything she asked for as far as sleeping pills were concerned. It seemed like pills were the norm back then.

Dr. Daz came and checked me over, and told Mum I had glandular fever. I wasn't very well at all. He gave Mum a prescription for some antibiotics, which were soon retrieved from the chemist. I was told to stay in bed and take two pills, four times a day.

By the next day, instead of feeling better, I felt terrible. Mum got a bit worried so went up the phone box to ring my boxing trainer, Johnny Gray. While she was gone, I stupidly sought out where her pills were, mistakenly thinking that if I took those as well as the antibiotics, then surely I will get better sooner. I found Mum's sleepers then foolishly took probably four or five of the red and white capsules. Mum came back and said that John was on his way.

By the time John had arrived, no more than an hour later, the pills I had swallowed had taken effect, and by now I was in an almost unconscious state. All I could recall were Mum and John saying, *"Look at Him, he doesn't look well at all!! I'll go and get his tablets."* I could barely understand what they were saying, but John said, "You better give him a good dose."

With that, *"Come on Paul,"* she encouraged, "Ge*t these down you sweetheart. They will do you the world of good."*

Clamping my mouth tightly shut, I mumbled through clenched teeth, something like, "No *Mum, please, I think I had enough of that, you will kill me!"*

In the end, I relented, and soon fell unconscious.

Obviously, my Mum, had the best intentions. She thought that my 'magic pill' was a cure for every ailment, and for everything really.

Thankfully, I woke up next day reeling from what could have been a fatal overdose.

A few days later, I was back on my feet and pursuing not just boxing but my criminal activities with the lads.

CHAPTER 11

Gosport Detention

If you think I would have learned my lessons from my Redhill detention, unfortunately I did not. Penal institutions can only do so much. It cannot change the heart. It cannot solve the root of the problem, which is our inherent tendency for wickedness.

Perhaps, by this time, you have nothing but hatred for me. It is fully understandable, but hang on, as it would get worse before it gets better and before I could be fully redeemed.

At 15, I began to be more daring. I was a full-blown criminal.

I had no respect for the law nor for other people's property or their feelings. I was selfish to the core. As I mentioned, Mr. Mischief, who became Mr. Destroyer, pursued me. I, along with the other lads would go around robbing houses, stealing cars, breaking into shops and on it went. I did whatever I liked, not caring for anything or anyone but myself.

Interestingly, sometimes, I was considerate. For example, in the middle of the night, I sneaked into the letter box of a house, we robbed, the photo I found in a locket. I thought, it had no value to me but it must have sentimental value to the owner.

Surely, I needed help. It wasn't long before enough was enough, not even the boxing club would come to my rescue.

I was a regular at Hastings Magistrates Court. Even the police officers and prosecution said, *"There is No hope for this boy. He needs serious detention or he would probably spend most of his life in prison."*

Indeed, I would soon be thrown to my next detention.

The Magistrate shook his head, as if to say, *"What a shame, what a waste, this boy has so much potential."*

I was given a 3-month sentence in a tough military detention centre at Gosport, in the south west of England.

"Take him away!" ordered the Magistrate.

I was led to the cells to await the prison bus, aptly called the sweat wagon.

Redhill Surrey Approved school was a holiday camp compared to this place. The only similarities were the castle like gates and high fences with sharp curled razor wires, which stretched for miles around the perimeters.

There was no slouching around in this place. You were on your own, each man for himself. Everything had to be done in military fashion on the double.

"Yes, Sir! No, Sir!" seemed like the only phrase permitted.

Any signs of disobedience were greeted with a slap across the face, which undoubtedly hurt.

And that was just for starters, because if that didn't work, you were then carted off to the block, stripped and slung into a bare cell for a couple of days.

That usually made us think twice.

It didn't take long to toe the line at Gosport. Every morning, the drill Officer with swagger stick under his arm came around and made sure that we were standing to attention, next to our beds. The beds had to be immaculately made with your kit neatly laid out on top of the bed. Shaped into a box, and without a crease to be seen.

Mine was a bit shabby this morning.

"Huggins! get down on your knees. I want twenty press ups. Now, boy! straighten that shirt up, lad!"

Then he walked to inspect the next bed. If you spoke out of turn, like I painfully found out, you were told to get on your knees and walk up and down the corridor with your feet off the floor.

I was totally humiliated when it happened to me. It wasn't long before this type of torture would leave you bleeding from the knee caps.

Out in the fields, and depending on the season, we would either plant or pick potatoes and we did that in silence.

Speaking out of turn, unless you were spoken to by an officer, was forbidden. As again, I found out the hard way.

"Huggins!"

"Yes, sir," I answered.

"Seems like you have lots of energy talking lad?"

"Yes, sir. I mean, no sir."

"See those heavy horse hair gym mats over their lad?"

"Yes sir," I said.

"See that football pitch, lad?" the Officer continued.

"Yes, sir," I replied.

"Go and grab the handle on that mat and drag it up and down the pitch, from goal post to goal post. I want to see you getting rid of some of that energy boy. Off you go, on the double," said the Officer.

I did what I was told until I could hardly stand any longer.

Looking over, the Officer blew his whistle, and then he called me.

Exhausted, I made my way back over to the potato field.

"How do you feel, Mr. Huggins?" said the Officer.

I felt like saying, *"How the effing well do you think I feel you bleep, bleep, bleep,"* but I wasn't brave enough.

"Get on with your work, lad, and not another word," instructed the Officer.

Day in day out was the same old routine: early morning bell calling us to get straight out of bed, then to our shower, breakfast, then bed dressing drill. Then we were out to the fields planting and digging in until noon. We'd take a break for dinner. Then back out again for hard labour, until tea time.

Then more gym drill. The gym Officer, Mr. Simpson, knew I was a boxer. He was a boxer himself. He would let me do boxing training in the equipment room. Mr. Simpson had his own bag hanging up in there. I was glad for the favoritism.

Gosport was a harsh disciplinary detention centre which was set out to install in us a respect for the law and to leave other people's belongings alone. And so, without any remission for good behaviour, I spent 3 long hard months at Gosport.

Johnny Gray, my trainer, came to pick me up.

It was a two hour or so journey back home to Hastings. John, who was like a father figure to me, spoke softly to me. He told me that I was one in a million, but if I didn't change, I would always have to pay for my crimes in this way. But if I was to behave, he told me what he believed, that one day 'I will be making good money as a boxing champion. Therefore, I should leave the crimes to the dogs.'

"No one likes a loser, but everyone loves a winner," he reminded me.

He always did his best for us boys at the West Hill boxing cub, and so did his wife, Gene. They even took me in for a few months, instead of being placed in another institution. They treated me like family.

Old Roar House

From staying at Johnny and Gene's for 3 months, it was decided by the Probation Board, and due to my continuous criminal activities with the lads, that it might be better if I was housed in a local children's home.

My new probation Office instructed me to go to the Hillcrest School gym and meet an Irishman by the name of Bill O'Rourke. Nothing else was said, only to go and see Bill. So, on the Thursday, as arranged, I went to see Mr. O'Rourke, who was himself a keen boxer, back in the day and trained at the West Hill Boxing Club.

Bill was a well-built man of about 5'10 inches tall, with thick curly, dark hair and a rugged face, and he was always smartly dressed. Bill called a 'spade' a 'spade', and you knew where you stood with him.

Bill ran the boxing and other sports education classes at Hillcrest school for children with social disorder and family problems. I did some pad work with him, which paved the way for a chat about my own troubled life in general.

After a good work out, I bid him goodbye and said, *"I hope I will see you again."*

Little did I know at the time that Bill was the headmaster at The Old Roar House, a children's home in St Leonards.

In retrospect, I was being vetted to see if I was suitable for a placement in his Old Roar Residency.

And so it was, Old Roar House was going to be my next home, and a good home too.

We had some good times at the O'Rourke's. They looked after us in there. The place was fully equipped with a tennis court, a swimming pool, even a five aside football pitch.

Unlike my times at the detention centres, I cherished my times at Old Roar House with the other boys and girls. We learned a lot too, mainly because we had to go to school.

At Christmas holiday time, Mr. O'Rourke and his wife, Teressa, organised performances for us in a number of care homes.

There, we would perform stage acts. I, with my friends, Tony Coleman and Phil Millen were in the black and white minstrel show. Mr. O'Rourke played the piano, 'mostly out of tune' and we boys would sing songs. We sang all the old second world war numbers which the residents loved. The girls would do dance routines and sung along too.

All in all, they loved us and we loved them.

Bill even got me a paper round up in the Ridge News agents. Bill's wife, Teressa, was an amazing woman and strong as an ox.

She did not hesitate boxing our ears, and she was good at it too. Colette and John, their kids, grew up with us.

Like in the Bembrook Road, we were one big family. There were no favorites.

Sadly, Old Roar House is no longer around.

Places like that, make a difference and give renewed hope. Genuine love, and not merely instilling hard discipline, certainly goes a long way.

The mouse plays

From Old Roar House, I was able to go home at weekends and as the saying goes, *'while the cat's away, the mouse plays.'*

Fishing especially in Alexandra Park was one of Broomgrove Estate boys' favorite past times. The boys included Lawrence Hale, Mark Stanbridge, Paul Jamison, among others.

Alexandra Park is said to have the largest population of tree species in Europe. It has beautiful, well-kept gardens, man-made ponds and small lakes with an abundance of birds and animal wild life throughout. The park is approximately one hundred and nine acres. Two of the ponds were designated for club members' fishing, but for the thrill, we preferred to fish at night in the ponds that says 'no fishing allowed'.

We went for the eels as they made a good saleable meal. Either we sold them in the Old Town fish market stalls, or Lawrence's mum cooked them for everyone to try. Jellied ells, yummy delicious!

During our weekend nights fishing in the park, we were alert. Before the police patrol car could reach us, we hid in the bushes, quietly watching them, as they, too, slowly crept past us.

Once they had gone, we scrambled back out to continue with our eel catching.

If we weren't eel fishing, you would find us playing cards over

One of the ponds in Alexandra Park.

at the St Helen's hospital waiting rooms. We found a special place where it was comfortable and undisturbed. When it got dark, and because I was the smallest, I would climb through the hospital store room window, where there were always plenty of Mackeson Stout bottles of alcohol we could steal and drink.

On other occasions, with our Yamahas, Suzukis, and Kawasakis, 50ccs, which, fifteen years old like me, were legally allowed back then, were led by the bigger boys, who owned 250 cc, out into the country lanes.

The 250cc lads zoomed up and down the Malvern Way Road, showing off the power of their machines as they clocked up speeds of 60 to 80 miles per hour.

One evening, our friend Jack Shoesmith was putting his helmet on ready to mount his 250cc flying machine, when out from nowhere one of the bigger bikes plowed straight into Jack. It launched him at least 7 feet into the air, and at the same time catapulting both Jack and the other biker 25 yards or so along the road.

Sparks flew in all directions. The biker got up almost immediately, but Jack laid motionless on the cold concrete, and an ambulance was called from the pub.

We surrounded Jack's motionless body and gently took off, with some difficulty, the damaged helmet. There was nothing, no movement and, worse still, no breathing.

"Come on Jack! Come on Jack! You can do it mate, please wake up," we quietly uttered.

Two to three minutes must have passed but we heard nothing from Jack.

Then, as if by a miracle, Jack exhaled the eeriest sound that I had ever heard. It was a deep groaning sound that just kept coming and coming, and then to our delight, he began to suck the air back in. Jack was alive.

The ambulance arrived within a few minutes. Jack was still laying on the ground unconscious, but he was breathing. The ambulance men gave Jack some oxygen, put him on a stretcher, and then took him away.

We saw Jack a week later in a pretty good shape.

Career choices

As much as I did not like school and could not wait for the weekends, school did not like me, either. I was almost in the bottom level of achievement classes. They went from class A, B, C, D and E, then the F troop. I was in the E group.

"You'll regret it, Huggins," said the teachers, *"When you get older, you'll wish you had tried harder. "*

So true were those words for me and for many. As I mentioned, early on, I cannot over emphasise the importance of a valuable education, whether in a formal school or just simply learning a trade. From a practical point of view, apart from actual knowledge and learning good conduct, getting a good education directs your career path or profession later on in life. For athletes like me, it could serve as a fall back, when things do not turn out as expected.

The school was relentless to make some sense out of me, though. Before my Secondary school ended, our careers teacher adviser, Mr. Max summoned me and asked me, *"What are you going to do, Paul when you leave school next year? Have you thought about your future occupation? You really can't be a clown all your life!"*

With pride, I said, *"I'm going to be a professional boxer, Sir."*

With a sigh, Mr. Max gently explained, *"I think you need to consider a more reliable source of income, young man. And besides, we don't do boxing lessons. Perhaps, you might like to consider the building trade. Let's be sensible, here. This is your future. We here at Priory Road want what's best for you."*

I had never thought of the future, but Mr. Max made me think that day, and encouraged me to do just that. Think! *"OK Sir, what about brick laying?"*

I thought of brick laying because I knew the school curriculum were offering building courses at Hastings College for one day a week. So, it was decided that the brickwork course was what I would do.

Satisfied and somewhat relieved, Mr. Max was happy that he had made at least some progress with me. But then, what would have been a normal college route turned into an organised criminal path, ending in prison.

Sixteen and my debut into the organised crime

During weekends, and when there was no school, I would get drunk and stoned with my friends half the time. There were pubs and nightclubs which would let us in, even though the doorman and pub staff knew we were nowhere near the legal age limit of 18 to purchase alcohol.

By the end of the school year, I had been introduced to some professional criminal activities. When I say 'professional criminal activities', I mean those organised by a syndicate. The syndicate targeted country mansions, which housed prized antiques. These antiques were sold either at auctions or abroad.

Since I was only 16, I mostly acted as a look-out. But one evening I got left behind. A police patrol car turned up just after a break-in, in the grounds of a country Tudor house.

It was pitch black, I couldn't see my way around so I hid and lay in the bushes. The officers were now out of the car and on foot with torches getting closer to my hiding place. I could hear them calling for the sniffer dog's assistance, as they could have a suspect within the grounds, which was me.

Approximately 15 minutes later, I heard from where I was concealed that the other police patrol dog unit had arrived. Their vehicle was only a few yards away from where I was lying in the wet brush. I had to hold my breath as the dog approached my hiding place. I lay there, terrified. as the sniffer dog was almost upon me. I could hear the beast sniffing at the undergrowth, just inches away from where my motionless body lay.

Maybe it was the sudden rain, which sent them away, or maybe the dog was not yet fully trained. I do not know for sure, but I was not detected. I stayed there for what must have been half hour or so, until at last both patrols departed.

"Phew! That was close," I just told myself.

I walked home counting my lucky stars.

I was wrong. My lucky stars did not last because I would soon be arrested, charged and be sent to prison.

My Barrister convinced the bench that I was just a pawn in the game, responsible for arranging the transport. Even so, that was enough to get me a 9-month prison sentence.

The first stop was to be Wormwood Scrubs Prison allocation holding cells, incarcerated in a small cell for a week. I was escorted away from Lewis Crown Court into a prison sweat wagon. The sweat wagons have little toilet-size cubicles where the prisoners are confined. I suffer from claustrophobia, so, it was a tough journey.

We were headed to another grown-up prison, where we waited for our proper placements.

At Dover

A week later at Wormwood Scrubs, I and some other inmates were allocated to our placement, Dover Borstal. We were given some prison kits and tobacco. All packed, we were then herded, to my great relief, into a more comfortable prison minibus. We set off from London Wormwood Scrubs to Dover.

The view to Dover was spectacular and after three hours or so, we reached the Dover Borstal or the Citadel, as it was known back then. Citadel was situated on top of the Western Heights in Dover.

Citadel later became a holding centre for immigrants who were caught mostly in the back of lorries at Dover docks. Then, finally, the Citadel closed altogether in November 2015. It now belongs to the English Heritage, mainly because it was also a strategic defense stronghold where German fighter airplanes were shot down in the Second World War.

On arrival and at the top of Western Heights, I could see a team of young men wearing black and bright yellow winter coats, who were clearing snow. Accompanied by prison officers, the young men were shoveling the deep winter snow away from what I learned later were the officers' homes.

It looked bleak up there, freezing cold and very miserable. And it was about to get even bleaker for many more months to come. We went through the same huge front castle gate and again down into a by now for me familiar reception area. At the Citadel Dover, the houses were all named after the Sussex and Kent Confederation of Cinque Ports: Dover, Hastings, Rye, Hythe, New Romney and Sandwich Houses. I was placed in Sandwich House.

For all the new arrivals, there was usually what was called a 'boot room inauguration bashing'. I never got one of those, but I did witness them a number of times. After breakfast, everyone in the work changing room would, on command from one of the head boys and without notice, all jump on the unfortunate inmate and basically give him a welcome boot bashing or to put it bluntly, a damn 'good kicking.'

After the rumble was over, everyone organised themselves outside the house into lines of five, with 10 in each line. This would take place every morning at 6:30 am, sharp.

Then from the whistle command, we marched in an orderly fashion in step for 5 minutes until we arrived in the morning parade yard. The morning parade yard was where every inmate from all the houses would gather each morning for our house roll call, just to make sure we were all still there.

My ears chimed when I heard the name Edmunds called out.

"Present, sir!" was the reply, and sure enough it was Phil from my home town, also a student at Priory Road. Phil was in Romney House.

It was a relief that, again, I knew someone from home. It made the homesickness a little more bearable.

Also, because I thought I needed a friend. My first encounter with one of the lads nearly ended in a fight

Rupert, his name was, asked me if he could have a roll up.

"Sure," I said, *"Take one,"* and handed him my quarter ounce pack.

He took it and began to indiscriminately shovel my tobacco into a cigar-size roll up.

"Are you having a laugh, mate?" I said. *"You' better put that back before we fall out."*

It got so heated that an officer had to intervene. It was sorted with us both getting a caution, and him without a roll up.

Though it was a long sentence, Citadel wasn't anywhere nearly as strict or harsh as Gosport. The prison officers didn't wear uniforms, but they all had their bunch of keys on a chain hanging from their belts. They had short or skinhead haircuts and they were all relatively easy going.

The food was not bad either with both a main course and pudding that came with a mug of sweet milky hot tea. We would sit in the dining room and just eat. I didn't say much, unless I was spoken to. There was always food left over from the serving hatch and would be given out on a '*rota system*'', so that everyone had their fair share.

After tea, we would take turns in doing the washing up. Then we could watch the telly or play games in the games room until 9pm, bedtime.

One Saturday evening, 'Butch Cassidy and the Sundance Kid' was on TV. It starred Paul Newman and Robert Redford. The film started at around 8.30 in the evening, but about fifteen minutes before 9 pm it would have been time for us to get ready for bed. We were enjoying the film so much that we had a vote and it was decided to barricade ourselves in the T.V. room and watch it till the end. A stupid thing to do, but it sounded like a good idea at the time. We held a brief meeting and it was decided. Those of us who didn't want to stay would leave the T.V. room.

Some left, probably, the sensible ones. Almost 20 young men between sixteen and nineteen-year-olds decided to stay. After the others left for their dormitories, we made sure the warden was out of sight, and then we piled together all the chairs we had against the T.V. lounge door to bar entry.

Defiantly, we all sat on the floor to watch the rest of the film. The Officers didn't seem bothered too much when our 9 pm bedtime bell rang. They peered in, got themselves comfortable chairs and just sat outside the T.V. room and waited. We rebellious young men thought we were the bee's knees as we laughed and smiled at the officers peering through the T.V room window.

We didn't watch much of the film. We were too busy laughing at the Officers, but we did not realise that the Officers would be getting the last laugh.

The film finished, but we stayed on until we soon got bored watching nothing. We decided to remove the chairs from the door and go to bed. But the officers had a better idea. The whistle blew and soon we were escorted outside, into the dark, cold parade grounds.

By now, it was way past midnight and bitterly cold with still remnants of the icy winter's snow etched around the grounds. Tonight, there was to be no cozy warm beds for us boys. We were on our way down to the block detention house. Ordered into lines of 5, and surrounded by guards. After the whistle, we were told to follow the leader in an orderly instep march.

As we made our way to the block house, the other house inmates were highly amused. They shouted, cheered and laughed from their barred dormitory windows as we marched by. It wasn't long before we reached the block. A name check was carried out. Then, we were ordered to strip to our underwear and shoved into the block house cells. There were so many of us in the block that night, that there weren't enough cells for each individual to go round. One in each cell was the usual procedure.

So, with no other choice, there were two or three of us locked into each cell.

After a sleepless night, we survived the cold cells with the biggest regret, because it added two more weeks to our time there. The Governor decided that an additional two weeks would be our final punishment.

It was by chance that the Officers did not know what we did when we were left on our own.

One of the boys called Johnson was in our dormitory of 6 lads in all. Every two weeks, Johnson had regular visitors who never missed throwing over the fence, in a designated spot, a small tin foil package in a cigarette box.

In the regular package drop was a good amount of cannabis resin. We would get high for 3 or 4 nights after Johnson's visitors. If we weren't smoking drugs, there were other substances I could get my hands on. I would sniff the workshop solvents or even drank the methylated spirits, which I found in the house cleaning stores cupboard. I only tried methylated spirit once and it sent me into hiding myself away in total panic. Just 10 to 15 minutes after drinking the foul substance and I was sure I was going to die. I felt as though I was disappearing down into a deep black hole. I went to my bed, feeling violently sick.

I tried that once and never again. It was so bad that I swore I'd never touch the stuff again, not even in desperate times. It was that bad.

Looking back, we had very little respect for each other. We were strangers in an institutionalised world. It was every man for himself.

Each week, we earned a few shillings so we could buy goods from the tuck shop, things like tobacco, packs of biscuits, bottles of squash, chocolates, toiletries and other bits and bobs. Yet, despite this luxury, we stole from each other's belongings if we had the chance to.

I saw one of the black lads, Leroy, put some stuff he stole into his bed locker. So, uninvited, and possibly to test him, I took a packet of his biscuits.

One of his friends saw what I did. It wasn't long before Leroy was confronting me in the upper landing wash room. There was nothing I could do but admit it, and basically said, *"So what if I did, what are you going to do about it?"*

Leroy was a solid built tough kid of probably seventeen years old. I knew he could handle himself as I'd seen him 'lick' (slap) one of the other bigger boys in another similar confrontation.

Leroy didn't respond, and just looked me in the eye for a second or two. Then, he unleashed a good solid left hook, which caught me flush square on the jaw. I hit the deck, dazed.

Fortunately, Officer Cameron was spotted by the lookout on his way down the corridor, which ended the fight abruptly. To take away the attention from ourselves, we both turned the taps on, pretending that we were washing.

To this day, I have two gold teeth, one on each side, as souvenirs of Leroy's hook. It was so hard, that it loosened a tooth each side of my jaw, exactly opposite each other. The Citadel Borstal's dentist kindly fitted me with two replacement gold teeth.

Despite my pride getting bruised, Leroy and I earned mutual respect for each other after that incident. We weren't really bullies, and we didn't take from the weaker boys.

And so, there it goes.

Every penal institution for the juvenile delinquents were different. Each had its own rules and varied activities, adopted either to tame you, keep you sane, teach or to just keep you alive.

Learning a trade at citadel

It was not all bad at Citadel. Citadel Dover Borstal was a learning centre as well as a correctional institution.

There were excellent work program opportunities in Citadel, which taught us, the inmates, a trade if we so desired. They came with a City and Guilds Certificate, to match.

I was determined to make use of my time well at The Citadel Dover Borstal with as much learning as possible. I knew it would make the time go faster and, of course, it would not hurt to get some sort of trade under my belt.

Mr. Bibbs was our house works coordinator. I arranged to meet him in his office and asked him if I could take part in one of the building trades courses. Mr. Bibbs told me, *"It just so happens that there is a spare place at Mr. Henshaw's plumbing class starting from Monday."*

Mr. Bibbs went on to say, "*The classes run every working day, Mondays to Fridays from 8 am after morning parade until 4 pm before tea time.*"

Remembering Mr. Max's counsel, I was delighted.

Mr. Henshaw was a jolly character who was probably in his late 50s back then. He was a stout man with gray hair swept across a bald head. Mr. Henshaw taught us everything about domestic plumbing and heating. He also taught us how to dress led and how to weld led and copper piping.

Our course lasted for 6 months, five days a week and we were doing 8 hours a day in the work shop. At the end of the course, we were presented with an Official City and Guilds Certificate from Dover College Institute.

At the end of each working day, the 4 pm bell rang to signal the last shift. We proceeded to our houses. I sometimes bumped into Phil, who was on the mechanics' course. We took the time to catch up and share a roll up before he went to his Romney house.

I treasured my daily chats with Phil, and, with the Plumbing course, time flew quickly.

Not long after, I found myself enrolled in what would be a continuation of my plumbing course at Hastings College.

CHAPTER 12

Back at home

At last, after almost 10 months at Citadel, it was time to go home and I was happy to be dressed in civilian's clothing too.

I was checked out at the gate. I was given my Plumbing City and Guilds Certificate and a decent amount of cash to tide me over. They also gave me a one-way train ticket to Hastings station.

I was so happy to be free. *"It's time for a fresh start*," I vowed.

Going back home on the train gave me time to reflect about where I was going from here.

I was almost 17. I thought of the West Hill Boxing Club. I was keen to get back to the sport. It was in my blood. Boxing was a part of my being and my family's too, who were my biggest fans.

The train stopped at Ashford station. I had to change trains for the Hastings line. Going past the stations from Rye and looking out across the fields, the fond memories of the days gone by came back to me. The countryside from Rye to Hastings is breathtaking. I wanted to get off to walk in the pastures that I'd missed for so many months, but I was yearning to see my Mum and family again.

My mind wondered back into the landscape, in which I loved so much to roam.

We were now going through the mile-long tunnel. It was dark in there. I was on my own in the carriage and could see my reflection in the train window. I looked away. I wanted none of my old self.

I reminded, myself, *"This is the new me."*

But I knew only too well that I was going to be in a constant battle with Mr. Destroyer.

This time, I would be prepared, I thought, and yet I knew, even back then, that it was and it would be, the toughest battle of my life. I truly wondered if I would ever be able to 'knock out my demons' by myself, and if my own efforts would be enough.

The train stopped at Ore station. I could have got off there, because it was the station closest to our home, but the sun was shining, and Mum wouldn't be expecting me until tea time. I hadn't seen the shops or the sea side for a long while, so I decided to get off at the next stop at Hastings.

Getting off the train, I crossed over the bridge. Ahead of me, there were many more bridges that I would have to cross, some bridges of tears, of pain, disappointments, and others that would lead me to some memorable achievements.

I passed my one-way ticket from Dover to the ticket master. It was so good to finally be home.

I made my way down to Hastings sea front. The midsummer's sun was high in the sky. People were ambling about, seemingly in no particular rush to get anywhere. It wasn't long before I bumped into someone I knew from my old school, Terry White.

"Hello stranger, where have you been?" asked Terry.

I told Terry that I'd been on holiday to H.M.P Dover, Borstal.

Terry bought me an ice cream, and wanted to know all about it. I told him as much as I could, but excluded the tears. Terry was satisfied that he would never want to be in such places, but continued, *"Hey at least you've got a City and Guilds, more than most of us have achieved."*

Terry left me to walk along the sea front. I stepped on to the beach and made my way over to the sea shore. The tide was out, and the kids were playing in the sand. There was a man digging lug worm. I went over to watch him. He was good at it, and already had a good few in his bucket. He said he was going to sell most of them to the fishing tackle shop, and the rest he would use for bait to catch bass, plaice and whiting off at Hastings Pier.

I thanked him for his time and began walking along the sand. I took off my jacket and shoes, and put them in my backpack.

As I ambled along and looking out to the deep blue sea, there was hardly a ripple that lapped on the sandy shore. It was so calm and serene.

There were fishing boats here and there, taking advantage of the fine weather. Sucking in the sea air, I picked up a flat stone and skimmed it across the top of the still waters. The stone caused a rippling effect. Watching it, I realised that it was like the story of my life so far. My actions always caused 'rippling effects', some good, but mostly bad.

"It was time to really change," I vowed to myself again.

With this resolve, I walked back home to our new and bigger council house at Quantock Gardens, still on Broomgrove Estate, which now had three bedrooms, instead of two.

I found out that my brother, Tony had got married to Sheila, who had a baby on the way. Our John had an extra job, part time, working with Oxo and Tosh in their commercial fishing boat, along with bottling up Saturday and Sunday mornings down at the Standard Pub, which was owned by a couple, John and Norma.

My youngest brother, Dean, was already a keen fisherman and also went out fishing with his Dad, Oxo, and Tosh. Dean, who's gifted intellectually, loved it more on the boats.

With all the fishing, we always had good fresh fish on the table with plenty of whelks and crabs.

I, on the other hand, after settling in, begun working with Hills and Pollington's Builders, as an apprentice plumber. It was a job that Trevor Bloomfield, a close kin of ours, had got for me. Trevor was a very good boxer too. Trevor was a painter and decorator who worked with Johnny Gray. His sons, Julian and Matthew, boxed at the West Hill Club as well.

Back at the club, there was talk of me, fighting my last amateur fight against the renowned, hard hitting, mature boxer, Johnny Shepherd.

After that, I was going to turn professional. I decided it was time that I start earning a living from a sport that I loved doing. I was confident that boxing was my future.

Before that, I'd developed into a man, almost overnight.

In where we lived, Dougie Scrase made an impact on my boxing as he consistently encouraged me to do well. He reminded me to not give up amidst the rigorous trainings and beatings. His son, Michael, became a boxer himself.

He and his wife, Jenny, were one of the kindest neighbours to me.

In life, we all need encouragers and people who genuinely believe in us. I had them, my family, my trainers and most of Hastings for support.

A disaster at college

Hills and Pollington was located at St. Leonards, Caves Road and I worked under Nobby Pollington, who was a lovely man. He was short, stocky, smoked a pipe and always wore a checkered lumberjack shirt and brown cord trousers. I have not seen anyone who smoked a pipe like Nobby. When he blew it, he sounded like he was blowing the horn. His favorite singer was Elvis Presley. Nobody could have been more upset than Nobby, the day that he found out that Elvis had died in August of 1977. He sent us all home that day as a mark of respect for the King.

Hills and Pollington Builders decided to send me to Hastings College, one day a week. I was to learn all that I could about plumbing.

Being at college was different from school. We called the teachers by their first names and we didn't have to wear our uniforms.

It wasn't long before I found out where my very own Plumbing classes discarded their scrap led and copper piping. 'A nice little unexpected flow of extra cash on tap'.

"Lovely," I thought.

The art of the game was not to raise suspicion, and keep what I was pilfering to myself, and never to take it all, leaving plenty behind. It worked, every time.

And just like that, my resolve to change vanished.

I liked it at college, and to be honest I barely played the clown. I think Mr. Max at Priory had talked some sense into me.

It was good to be mixing with the opposite sex, too. Priory Road was an all-boys school. You had to be a boy's boy, but hey, now I could be a girl's boy as well.

But I wasn't much good at it. Not only was I too immature for my age, but believe it or not, I was not confident when it came to girls. I had a girlfriend when I was almost 15 though, and her name was Tracy. Along with my Mum, Tracy used to watch me box. Both of them, cheering me loudly in the audience.

I liked Tracy a lot. We only kissed. I was too shy to try anything else, and besides back then, sex was a taboo at that age. I wish I could tell you that I remained awkward towards the opposite sex, but I did not. Due to drugs and alcohol, I found myself many mornings with one-night stands. After Tracy and at 18, the only girl I had a serious relationship with was Jessica. But regrettably I was

KNOCKING OUT MY DEMONS

violent towards her when drunk and drugged up and she left me after I beat up her male friends due to my irrational jealousy. Later in life, I had relationships with various, well-meaning women and fathered six children. Out of respect, this is the chapter in my life I chose not to delve into.

College did not last long for me, because of an impending disaster caused either by sheer ignorance or outright foolishness.

After a month or so, I and my classmate, Alfie Apps, were designated by our plumbing class master, Mr. Drinkwater, to put in the new radiators in the two new office rooms being constructed in the college.

Our primary task was to fix the radiators to the walls and then connect the pipework to the main flow and header tank in the College's roof.

I was told to turn off the main, downflow gate valve, which was connected to a two-inch steel downflow pipe, which in turn was connected to a one-thousand-gallon feeder tank.

I made my way up into the roof top. I managed to find the light switch and turn the lights on. I was armed with a monkey wrench and hammer. I found the gate valve connected to the huge water tank, but when I tried to turn it off, it wouldn't budge because it had rusted solid, over the years.

So, I gave it a few light taps with the hammer.

"Let's try, that," I confidently proclaimed.

I must have hit it a little too hard, because after a couple of whacks, the valve snapped clean off from the base of the huge tank full of water. The force of the gush exploded full onto me and almost knocked me sideways. The water shot out through the roof hatch then began cascading down the collage's stairwell.

Other students with their class masters who were then leaving their classrooms below, held their books as the water splashed down through the ceilings.

The flow to the tank was turned off by an astute woodwork teacher. The tank was made safe, before the whole thousand gallons were emptied from the tank. The woodwork teachers came up with the bright idea to hammer home a piece of two-by-two wood, that was shaved down to fit into the hole.

My mess was sorted over a span of 4 or 5 minutes. It was to become the beginning of a near end of my plumbing career, as it wasn't the last flooding, I was responsible for, either.

Thankfully for the College, and everyone's sake, I soon gave up after the second disaster.

I decided it would be wise, if I stick to boxing.

My Last Amateur Fight. With my trainer, Johnny Gray and Manager, Dave Harris.

CHAPTER 13

My last amateur fight

And so, I was about to fight John Shepherd, the ABA Southern Counties Champion form Dartford, Kent.

I had seen John fight. He was two or three years older than me, with a strong chin and not an ounce of fat on him. He trained hard and fought to win, at all costs. I was in for a war.

I was delighted because it was going to be staged in Hastings, obviously, my home court. Fighting in front of my home crowd was always exhilarating, to say the least. For me, it was always a chance to please my townmates. As far as I can remember, I never lost at home.

More importantly, I was committed to leave the amateur level with a win. I had a good record in the amateur level. By the time I was 16, I had won 47 out of my 50 or so contests, and accumulated a lot of silverware from the victories.

Now was the time to show that I had what it takes, 'when needed', to do the job at hand. I badly wanted to show my future manager that I had the magic bullet in both hands along with my mental strength to overcome the temptations, which were always crouching in the shadows. willing and able to draw me away from the illustrious prizes of future success.

As clear as the daylight, I had an addictive personality, which often would get the better of me, and with fatal consequences. But this time, I refused to bow down to my addictions. I took the initiative to set the goals for myself.

At 16 with my accumulated trophies.

My favourite regular venue to fight at home was Hastings Pier. A close second was the Queens Hotel ballroom, where I fought John in the spring of 1980, the month of March.

That night in the Queens Hotel, I weighed in at Bantamweight, which is 8 stone and 6 pounds. John Gray, my trainer and Dave Harris would be in my corner.

I was getting near 19, and I was beginning to fill out a bit. I was also becoming a more matured, harder puncher. I had a few more months to gain the weight and qualify for the featherweight's division of 9 stone, 4 pounds.

The show was a sell-out but that night, of course, my Mum, together with our John, were my greatest fans.

Just before my fight, in the dressing room, I shadow boxed and hit the hands of my trainer Johnny, with super-fast combinations. Heart pounding, as always.

Johnny Sheppard was already in the red corner, eagerly waiting and ready for the contest to begin. I had been prepped well back in the dressing room, and the adrenaline was pumping throughout my entire body. I knew that I had it all to win. Johnny weighed in at a few pounds heavier than me, which was normally the case for most of my fights. I was always described as 'pint sized' in the papers.

It was going to be a tough fight, and to make it worse the pressure was all on me. Jimmy McSweeney, the Master of Ceremonies announced that this was my last amateur contest. Jim then went through the other formalities such as how much we weighed, the clubs we belonged to and what championships we had both won.

I cannot remember much of the fight, except the momentous moment when I sustained a cut under my right eye during the second round. The referee had to momentarily stop the fight, so I could be examined. But the fight continued.

And the roars of encouragement around the arena motivated me to stay on my feet. I tucked in and began to pummel my opponent's body, then switching to send crashing left and right hooks to John's head. I remember that I just needed to stay close and push Johnny backward, sending him off balance.

The next round was the last round with final instructions from John to stay on my front foot and to push forward.

After 3 hard fought exhausting minutes, the bell sounded that ended the fight. I knew I'd done enough to win. We were taken to the centre of the ring.

I won the fight on a unanimous decision from the judges.

The crowd erupted with cheers and I had once again proved to myself, to my team and my home crowd that I had the ability, the strength, and the focus to be in the higher league.

That is, if Mr. Destroyer, who I had managed to ignore for this fight, would not strike and get his revenge.

CHAPTER 14

The drunken and disorderly boxer

We are creatures of habits, and that includes distractive habits.

We also have established routines, even for leisure, pleasure, or as the learned would call it, recreation.

During the summer of that year, 1980, on Sunday mornings, Dad, myself, Tony, Phil Barker and sometimes joined by Gunner Page, would go out to the Sussex and Kent country fields.

The farmers used to call the rabbits 'field rats', but for us they were dinner. We also sold them in the local pubs, and they were always a sell-out.

Sometimes, we obtained the farmer's permission to enter his land, though mostly we did not bother. I learned to cover up our number plate with clumps of wet mud and straw.

In one of our field trips, Dad had a fight with a farmer and we all had to make a quick getaway in the van with the dogs, rabbits and all. By the time the 'not too happy farmer' got back to his feet, we had sped off.

Once out at Winchelsea, Tony's lurcher cross greyhound had gone missing, and he'd found out that the farmer had shot it and threw 'Old Kit' into a skip.

The most memorable one though, ended me in the headlines.

Tony wasn't feeling too good, because of too much unnecessary chemicals in his system. He felt he needed to get out into the wilderness for a few days. So, he asked me if I would join him. Of course, I did. It sounded like fun, camping out for a few days while Tony got his head together.

We packed our rucksack with two sleeping bags, a frying pan, a couple of tins of beans, a tin opener, a rabbit skinning knife and an axe. We took along with us his dog, Musket, and the ferret.

The first day went by nicely. We ended up in a field out at Doleham Halt. There were some rabbit earths visible and our dog, Musket, told us that it had occupants. Covering up the five or so holes with our nets or flops, as we called them, we'd then put the ferret down one of the rabbit holes. We backed off and just let the ferret do its job, which was to chase the rabbits that were in the earths until they bolted out into the nets. After that, whoever was closest, would fix onto the rabbit and swiftly break its neck.

That night, for dinner, we had fried rabbit stew with some herbs which we found growing in the field. Cooking it on a beach wood open fire made it more delicious. We lay in our sleeping bags, staring up into the magnificent cloudless night, as the shooting stars flickered across the glittering sky.

Even as a child, the experience of nature, day or night, was so overwhelmingly amazing, that I had never dreamt of living in a big city. In fact, I recall that I wanted to continue boxing, not only for my personal accomplishment, but to be able to earn enough money for a house and a big garden in the country.

In the morning, Tony and I, Musket and the ferret finished off the stew. From Doleham Halt we walked to Winchelsea beach, where we chanced upon an empty holiday caravan chalet. I tried the door and to our delight found that it wasn't locked. We spent our second night in the chalet.

We ate well, too. There were some cans of food, which the last occupants left behind and a few coins from the electric meter, which we grabbed for our supplies.

So far, our alcohol and drug free adventure was going well. Until expedition day three, that is. The next and final stop of our adventure was Rye.

We had both done well in keeping ourselves sober for the past two days but upon reaching the High Street of Rye, the sight of the Off License got the better of us. All that was needed was the whisper from Mr. Destroyer and I rushed to the store faster than 'Jack Robinson'.

Tony went to the counter and asked the shop keeper for some Old Holborn tobacco. When the shop keeper had turned around for the tobacco, I slipped a bottle of brandy down the front of my trousers. We both then left and made our way up the High Street and out towards Iden, which is a mile or so from Rye's town centre. I reached into my trousers and produced the brandy, dangling it in front of Tony's nose. It was like handing sweeties to a baby. We downed the bottle almost immediately. And after that, we wanted more.

We found our way back to the High Street pubs, where we stopped at the George Inn. George Inn was a very pleasant, up-market establishment. In addition to our musty smell, my brother and I looked out of place dressed like tramps, but we did not care.

We had our dog and the ferret, which were now loose and running around in the bar.

By this time, the brandy had got hold of us and Tony began singing and dancing about the place. We were beginning to arouse quite a bit of attention. Until finally, it was the last straw when Tony got the axe out and embedded it into the beautiful oak open fireplace exclaiming that it would be useful for our camp fire that evening.

The police soon arrived. We were promptly ordered to get our animals under control and to leave the premises. I apologised as best I could, then we staggered off out down the road to the next pub called The Standard.

Before entering the Standard, we tried to pull ourselves together. I ordered the drinks, *"Two halves of your finest country ale, please."*

I went and put a coin in the jukebox and choose a Dr. Feel Good number called 'Milk and Alcohol,' to Tony's delight. He proceeded to leap and somersault around the bar floor. It wasn't long before the police were once again called and we found ourselves leaving with a final warning.

Stubborn, intoxicated and bolder, we made our way to the bottom of the street and found ourselves in the Pipemakers Arms. This was more like our cup of tea. Or should I say, 'Director's Ale' The 'Pipemakers' was a spit and sawdust pub, which catered to the local bikers, fishermen and other such characters who all enjoy a good drinking session. This pub had a great jukebox and we were soon rolling around the floor. The dog was chasing our ferret around the bar and Tony once again thought it was a good idea to use his axe in one of the tables. It wasn't long before Tony almost cleared the bar with his crazy drunken antics, which to me, back then, were hilarious.

The police turned up again and demanded that we leave town. Not too happy with this, Tony in his drunken state then shouted, *"We're not going anywhere!"* and at the same time he staggered towards the very large police officer with his axe waving in the air.

This was the last straw. Tony was wrestled to the ground and immediately, handcuffed.

Ten minutes later, we were both locked up inside the cells of Rye Police Station. The police took the dog and ferret and put them in the back of the police station.

In the morning, we were both charged with 'drunken disorderly behaviour with intent to cause criminal damage.' Because Tony was so drunk, the kind police officers decided that they would not push for the more serious charge of possession of a dangerous weapon with intent. We were swiftly discharged from the police station, probably because we smelt so bad, but before we could have our animals back, we had to pay ten pounds for overnight kennel charges.

With not a penny between us except enough change for a phone call, along in the call box we rang Dad up to come and get us. And then we added, *"Please bring ten pounds to get our beloved pets released."* Dad was not pleased at all, but he came.

That weekend, I made the headlines in the local papers, saying, *'Up coming boxing star: drunk and disorderly.'*

During the hearing at the Rye Magistrates Court, we had to listen to the charges against us. As the prosecutor read out the shenanigans leading up to our arrest, I found myself recounting the details, all in my mind, of the singing, dancing, chopping, axe waving, dog and ferret roaming, to the point and to my brother's horror, I just burst out laughing. I could not help it.

The Judge looked at me sternly and warned, *"I'll be giving you something to laugh about in a minute, Mr. Huggins!"*

To our surprise, the Judge was friendly, after all. He commended me for my past achievements in boxing. He added that I was to seek help from an assigned Social Disorder Probation Officer. He also gave me a hefty fine of £250.

Tony also got off lightly, with a two-year suspended prison sentence, and a fine equal to mine. And if we were together, we were also banned from visiting Rye.

I decided that my fine was too much to pay, just for having a good night out in the town. So, I promptly appealed my conviction.

The Lewis Crown Court reduced my fine to fifty pounds on the grounds of me being misled by my older brother.

My Barrister wanted £60 as compensation for loss of earnings and as reimbursement for the travelling expenses to court from Hastings.

Our shameless plea was objected profusely by the prosecution.

CHAPTER 15

The launch of my professional boxing career

I thought plumbing was something I could fall back on but I shelved it so I could focus on my boxing career. I knew that the professional league is a world apart from the amateur game and needed total commitment.

Dave Harris and I sat down and had a long 'man to man' talk. As timely as my professional debut at 19, Dave was about to take his Professional Boxing Manager and Trainer licence exams. Dave wanted to sign me up.

I took the offer. Dave, was not only a well-known boxer trainer in town but I had a feeling he would always look after my best interest. He also didn't want to take the full manager's fee that he was entitled to.

I was also delighted that he had arranged for me to be trained by one of the most well-respected trainers in the London circuit, Frank Duffett.

When the day came for me to go to London to get my professional boxing licence from the British Boxing Board of Control, I was both extremely excited and nervous. Basically, to be given a licence, I needed to get in the ring and do three or four rounds of boxing with another seasoned professional. The assessment was to be held at the Thomas a Becket gym. The gym was above the pub in the Old Kent Road, London, and in those days was home to Henry Cooper, the former British, European and Commonwealth heavyweight champion, who trained at the premises six days a week. Other great fighters had at, one time in their careers, used the gym in preparation for their fights; to name a few: Muhammed Ali, Joe Frazier, Sugar Ray Leonard, Roberto Duran and on it goes.

I passed with flying colours. My past record spoke for itself. All went as planned and my first professional fight at nineteen was arranged at the World Sporting Club in the prestigious Grosvenor Hotel, Park Lane of London on 15th September 1980. I was to fight Steve Farnsworth.

Steve was a capable fighter, a Sheffield lad, who was 5 ft 11 inches tall and weighed in at super featherweight. This meant that he had a good long reach and a few pounds in weight and height advantage over me.

Of course, both Dave and I wanted to start my professional debut with a win, and so we trained hard.

The prize money was not too bad, either. The purse for fighters back then when starting off was more or less £600 for a six-round contest.

Dave and I were also given a hundred tickets or so for our Hastings fans, which along with Mum and John, we used to have a coach load up to London. The presence of my Hastings

townmates was always of great comfort to me as I knew that I was not entirely alone in my fights.

My fight went the six rounds distance with the durable Steve but we were all very pleased with the outcome. I won, almost unscathed.

At the Grosvenor Hotel dinner shows, I normally met some famous people.

On this professional launch, I had impressed Sir John Mills, the film

Dave and my champion belt.

actor who starred in over 120 films. One of his films was the memorable 1946 'Great Expectation' movie from the Charles Dickens novel. John played Pip. So pleased with the contest, he came to me, handed me some 'pocket money' and reminded me to train hard and to keep my eyes on the goal.

Hastings & St Leonards Observer, Sat September 20 1980

OBSERVER SPORT - news and action

Paul Huggins ducks a left from Steve Farnsworth.   Huggins pins his man in the fourth round.   "I've done it."

A GREAT PROSPECT, SAY THE EXPERTS

PAUL CLOSE TO A QUICK KILL

PAUL Huggins, the tiny terror of Hastings boxing, launched his professional career in triumph this week. And the experts agreed: He's a great prospect.

The 19-year-old former national schoolboy champion from the Broomgrove Estate stepped into the ring at London's World Sporting Club at 10.25 on Monday night.

He emerged 20 minutes later sweating and shattered, but successful and almost unscathed after six gruelling rounds.

Appearing as a total unknown on Paddy Byrnes' show and down in the programme as Charlie Huggins, he ripped into action with all the sophistication of an out-of-control express train. But he soon proved he was no Charlie.

Confident and single-minded, he summoned a

Story: Philip Elms
Pictures: Jim Redman

crescendo of noise from the 700 dinner-jacket crowd at Park Lane's Grosvenor House when it looked as if the referee might intervene in the fourth round to save fancied featherweight Steve Farnsworth from further battering.

But relief for the Sheffield man came in the form of the timekeeper's bell.

Farnsworth had twice come close to dropping as the eager Huggins piled on the aggression, but the Hastings man failed to connect with a couple of potentially killer punches.

The Sheffield boxer was having only his second professional fight, yet he was already a man with form. In his debut he beat Britain's 25-rated featherweight Selwyn Bell, who has had 49 contests.

Farnsworth came good in the last two-minute round, but a shattered Huggins had done his job and the referee

immediately held his arm aloft.

He scored Huggins 60 points, Farnsworth 58, making Huggins a clear winner of four rounds.

Amid screams of great jubilation Huggins supporter Dave Reedon leapt into the ring and picked up the young winner.

The MC described the fight as "a wonderful contest" and film star Sir John Mills, suitably impressed, decided to give each fighter £25.

DELIGHTED

Henry Cooper and Terry Lawless were among those to acknowledge the Huggins potential.

Delighted trainer Frank Duffett called him "the greatest fighter to come out of Hastings since William the Conqueror — and he was unbeaten in Europe."

Paul's mum, Rose, thought

her boy was "great, fantastic."

But in the calm of the dressing room, manager Dave Harris and trainer Duffett told Paul he must tighten his defence, stop the early head-hunting and go for body punches.

Said Harris, who has yet to secure his manager's licence: "I was very pleased and glad he went the full route.

"I am hoping he can build up a good reputation and a winning one."

Huggins, a former Priory Road schoolboy, will learn soon enough that professional boxing is a world apart from the amateur game, but his prospects are bright.

On the strength of Monday's victory Huggins was invited to appear at the National Sporting Club next week.

But manager Harris turned down the invitation as the fight followed so soon after his debut contest.

Another London offer has also been turned down and Paul's next scheduled fight will be at Hove Town Hall on October 20. Coaches are being laid on for local supporters.

Congratulations from Sir John Mills and show promoter Paddy Byrnes.

Back in the dressing room victory is shared by manager Dave Harris (left) and trainer Frank Duffett.

The Observer's report on the night.

On another occasion, Muhammad Ali just turned up out of the blue to promote his book 'When We Were Kings,' which caused a bit of a stir. It was a surprise appearance, and I went to shake his hand.

Later in my career, I met other famous world boxing champions.

After the fight, I was praised in the local papers and earned the nickname, 'Fireball', for being fiery. The experts described me as a 'great prospect'.

The Hastings Old Town Fishing Community

Of course, boxing is not your usual every day work. I had to train six days a week as a boxer to keep myself fit and strong but fights are matched and planned.

My boxing record showed that I had 33 professional fights, the first 15 fights of which, I was unbeaten. I will focus on my most memorable fights in the next few pages of this book.

Despite the lack of a regular job, I never went without in the Old Town. Hastings is full of the most generous people on the planet, and still is today.

I lived on the out skirts of the Hastings Old Town fishing community. As a youngster, I have always enjoyed fishing.

And so, when I needed some spare cash or a good feed of fish, I was always welcome to go out with the fishing lads.

Sometimes, I got up at 3 in the morning and made my way down to the inshore fishing fleet. Out there, we might be either trawling or hauling our trammel nets.

Back in the day, the Hastings Old Town fishing fleet was recognised as being the largest inshore fishing fleet in Europe. In shore, this meant that we did not need to go out to sea any further than 7 or so miles. Any further than that was considered dangerous because you were in the main shipping lanes.

Hastings fishing community.

There were times we had some near misses as the enormous tankers and cruise ships steamed passed in the dead of night. They sounded out their horns on approach, once they spotted us on their radars. We were just yards away as the steel mountains passed by, steaming on to their destinations.

As they passed us by, our little boats in comparison would bob up and down in the wake of the ships.

I immensely enjoyed fishing with the lads, the Edmunds', Dave the dog, the Hamiltons, Obie, and David Kirtly.

Dave and his family treated me well. I love them all.

Jekkyl and Hyde

But while I was Paul 'Fireball' Huggins in the ring, I was 'Jack the Lad' on the streets. It was the classic Jekyll and Hyde personalities.

At 20, I was still unbeaten in 12 of my professional fights and I mistakenly and arrogantly assumed that I was unstoppable.

Before one of my fights, with Richie Foster, I was out with my friends. After the club closed at 2 am, we ventured to a joyride in my little Morris car.

We were drunk and I was driving, but I did not care nor mind any potential damage or death we could cause. I just drove like mad around town, even laughing to our hearts' content.

As I drove up Old London Road, and then turned left at the top of the hill and down Frederick Road to take my friends home, I heard Mr. Destroyer whispering, "*Go in to the woods, instead.*" And I did, just that. Doing a hard left, the car span into the entrance of St Helens woods. Hooting the horn and flashing the lights and laughing like a lunatic, I was like a man possessed until we landed in a ditch and could go no further.

With that, I cried out without a care in the world, "*That's it, lads it's all over.*"

Sobering up somewhat, I continued, "*That's the end of the party, I'm afraid. We'd better get home before the police turn up.*"

And so we walked, separately, in darkness, towards, the direction of our respective homes, and me with my dog.

After a hundred yards or so, I realised that I had left a set of golf clubs back in the car. I didn't want to lose them, so I went back with my dog Lucy to get them. Sure enough, there they were in the boot.

As I put the clubs over my shoulder, I noticed torch lights and the sound of voices towards the entrance of the woods. The police had turned up and they had brought their friend with them, a very large Alsatian sniffer dog.

"Now, this was going to be tricky," I realised.

I needed to get through to the other side of the woods to reach home with my clubs and my dog, as quickly as possible.

The friendly Alsatian had sniffed out Lucy and headed towards our direction. I decided to run as quick as I could before the Officers could see me.

The moon was brightly shining, so I could see my way reasonably well. The ground was slippery and muddy as it had been raining earlier that evening, but I saw lights at the other end. The two dogs were having a grand time.

Getting through the other side, I quickly ran up the bank to our Quantock Gardens block of flats. I left Lucy with her new found friend, still bounding around together.

By that time, I was covered in mud. I saw that Mum's downstairs neighbour Margaret's light was on, and so I banged on her door. She opened it. I rushed in.

"It's Ok, Margaret, its only me. I just need to take my clothes off," I explained.

Before Margaret had a chance to reply, I burst out, *"The police are chasing us. It's my car. I'll explain later."*

I then quickly whipped off my top and muddy trousers, my socks and shoes, then ran back out of Margaret's house and up the stairs to the house. I quickly opened the front door, went in and found some fresh pyjamas and put them on as fast as I could.

By the time I'd tidied myself up and put the kettle on, there came a loud knock at the front door. I went and opened it and there standing in front of me were the scruffiest, muddiest looking two police officers I had ever seen.

"My goodness, me!" I exclaimed. *"What on earth can I do for you, Officers? You look like you could do with a cup of tea, please do come in,"* I added.

The Officers looked me up and down with their torches, in disbelief. Our furry friends were sitting nicely outside the door panting away with their tongues hanging out.

"*There you are, Lucy! Where on earth have you been all night? Look at the state of you!*" I stressed.

"*Where is your car, Paul?*" asked, the muddy Officer.

I went out onto the balcony and looked over into the parking bays. "*It's down there somewhere Officer, Sir.*" I replied.

With that, the both of them, echoed, "*You know where your car is Paul. No doubt we will be seeing you again. Only next time, we will make sure that we catch you.*"

They then walked off.

"*Now, come inside Lucy, you naughty girl.*"

Regrettably, back then, I thought the world was one big playground.

CHAPTER 16

Some of my most memorable professional fights

The first fight with Richie Foster

As mentioned, I was matched to fight Richie Foster, a man from Dublin, who I was told became the Amateur Commonwealth Games Champion. With that in mind, I resolved to put more effort into training, instead of 'clowning around' in town.

For most of my professional fights, my poor trainer and manager, Dave, struggled to keep me on a straight path but he could only do so much. I was my own worst enemy, and the toughest opponent I ever fought with was myself and the ever so crafty, Mr. Destroyer.

Anyways, the fight was set to take place at Hove Town Hall, Sussex on 12th January 1981. Apart from fooling around and nearly getting locked up for drunken and dangerous driving, I spent much of my time before the fight selling tickets and generally promoting my own fights. I loved doing it, especially that we lived in a small town, where almost everyone is acquainted with each other.

I was always determined to get the coach full, as that meant an extra hundred pounds or so added to my meager 600 pounds purse. Mind you, back then, the cost of living was less expensive. You could buy a pint of beer for 59 pence. A litre of fuel cost around 28 pence and a loaf of bread for 27 pence.

The fight with Richie turned out to be a good show for the crowd. The town hall was packed.

I was a strong and aggressive, an all-action fighter who punched well above my weight and I was also a show man. I would smile as I demolished my opponents to the canvas. I would stand over them, grinning and taunting them to get up and fight. Merely for the show.

The bell sounded for the first round. I rushed to take control of the centre of the ring from where I could dominate the fight. The crowd were chanting *"Huggy! Huggy! Huggy!"* Richie was a tough and very fit man and it felt like I was punching a man of steel.

Round after round, we stood toe to toe. Not one of us stepping back, we were crashing body and head shots at each other till the very end. It was one of those matches that lifted the roof off the building. The sound coming from Hove town hall was a phenomenal experience.

Derek Leaney, the Brighton commentator described the fight as one of, if not the best, he had ever commentated. The final bell drew a rapturous applause for us both, and the nobbins showered into the ring. The referee had no other choice but to raise Richie's and my hands as a draw.

My share of the goodwill gesture thrown into the ring came to well over one hundred pounds.

One year and almost two months later Richie and I would fight again at my favourite boxing arena 'The Royal Albert Hall' in London. I only lost once out of my 9 fights in the Royal Albert Hall.

In the second fight with Richie, I was better prepared and was in a better shape both mentally and physically.

That night, I came home with the winning prize.

The Don Cockell's charity event

Don Cockell fought the great heavyweight champion, Rocky Marciano on the 15th of May 1955.

I had the privilege to meet Don Cockell in his own cancer charity night.

Don used to own the Jenny Lind pub in Hastings and my Dad drove for him after he retired from boxing.

Don was suffering from throat cancer and had fallen on hard times. The fighters came from as far as America, with the likes of Floyd Patterson, Henry Cooper and Billy Walker, along with other celebrities. It was a well-attended event, to say the least.

I was topping the bill that night, defending my Southern Area title against Rory Burke. Harry Carpenter was the commentator for the fight and the event was shown on the Grandstand sports channel.

In the first round, I had broken my right hand.

I told Dave, who was also my corner man, when I'd sat on my stall after the bell: *"Dave, I've broken my right hand."*

Dave replied, the obvious, *"Don't worry, Paul, just use the other one!"*

This is boxing, after all. You've got to fight to live.

After being declared winner after the 7th round, I saluted Don.

We raised around £11 thousand for Don, that night. Not bad, for a brave, old Champion, who deserved every penny.

An early night: The fight with Peter Gabbitas

Like Richie, Peter Gabbitas was an Amateur Boxing Association British Champion, and was 2 years older than me.

At that time of the fight, Peter had won 5 out of his 6 professional contests. It was my goal to make it 5 out of 7.

The fight took place on 2nd March 1981 at the Corn Exchange, in Brighton.

The hall was packed and Peter and I were picked to fight first. I did not know that my supporters had just arrived as I got into the ring.

Names and weights announced, the bell sounded for the first round while the Hastings bunch were in the bar, having a few drinks.

Like a wild, hungry animal which had spotted blood, I tore into my opponent with relish. I took no prisoners, and threw shots from all angles, most of them hitting both body and the head. I did not give Peter the chance to hit back.

The referee had no choice but to stop the fight in only thirty-six seconds into the first round.

By the time, most of my fans came back into the hall, it was all over. Though they did not get to see the fight, they were very much pleased with the result.

I wished they had seen me though.

Fight after fight, everywhere

For the first few years of my professional career, I had a continuous victorious run. I managed 2 draws in 15 contests and none lost.

I later won draws both from Richie Foster and Steve Cleak on our return bouts. Steve Cleak was the Welsh featherweight, from Porthcawl. I told him during the weigh-in that I would knock him out in the second round. It happened, on the 19th of January 1982 in the Royal Albert Hall.

As mentioned, the Royal Albert Hall was special to me.

Before my fight with Steve and also at the Royal Albert Hall, I beat the more experienced boxer from Manchester, Ian Murray. It was also a quick win for me in the second round. In the few minutes of the fight, I could not find my range and Ian flicked out long left jabs, but then I found my bearing and started punching closely to the body. I scored with two right hands in the first round.

Knocking out Steve Cleak.

In the second round, Ian fell, but recovered. Then I remember hitting him really hard with a left hook on the body, and he fell again. This time, while he desperately tried to get up, he failed. The referee took up the count and I won on TKO.

On my way up the rankings ladder, I also had fought and had beaten John Feeney, who had once held the much-coveted prize in British boxing as a British Champion, 'The Lonsdale belt'. With the victory, also came the hard losses. I lost a total of 9 fights, two of them to Pat Doherty, but previously I had stopped Pat in 4 rounds.

Fight with Pat Doherty.

I also lost too but again I'd beaten Clyde Ruan, other foreign opponents and of course to World Champion, Barry McGuigan.

In 1982, as I was in Glasgow, I saw Steve Sims in his British Championship fight and, being the showman I was, I shouted after he won the fight that I would fight him anytime, anywhere.

The fight was finalised but never materialised. Thirty-one years later, in 2014, when I was living in Newport in Wales, I and Steve got re-acquainted. He came to the house for tea with the Contract, which he wanted me to sign, for old time's sake. We had a good laugh. I became a regular in his gym and he even came to church with me.

The fight that never was, with Steve Sims.

For now, allow me to carry on with the last few highlights of my boxing career, hoping that if you are not a boxing fan, you would not find it too boring.

Barry McGuigan

I'm going to be honest and yes, even management can make big mistakes. Personally, I think my management made an unforeseen mistake staging this fight for two reasons. First, I was not in the right frame of mind to fight because of personal issues I was dealing with. Second, the fight was to take place in Belfast.

To win a fight in Barry's homeland would not be an easy feat. My Manager was warned against taking the fight by the more experienced Barrett and Duff promotions, but we went ahead. Oh well, I was not exactly faultless, because I was too proud to admit that I was not ready for the fight.

In hindsight, I should have refused until I felt the time was right and in my favour. But, maybe, my Manager really believed I was up for the fight against Barry, considering that I had beaten an opponent of Barry, not once, but twice. Peter Eubanks had beaten Barry on the 3rd of August 1981 at the Corn Exchange Brighton. The logical possibility is that if I could beat Peter, who beat Barry, then I could beat Barry too. But hey, everything is a possibility in this world, right?

The day before our fight on the 8th November 1982, we were met at the airport by the McGuigan team. After the formalities, we were then taken to our hotel, 'The Europa' in Belfast. Back then the Belfast streets were occupied with British troops because the UK was trying to regain control of Northern Ireland from the Irish Republican Army (IRA). The IRA wanted reunification of Ireland.

Sparring with Mark West, in preparation for the fight.

Anyways, we were about to fight our own battle in the famous, Ulster Hall. The Hall was a venue for entertainment and is situated in the City of Belfast. Handel's Messiah heralded the opening of the Ulster Hall in 1862.

The night before the fight, I thought it would be just fine to pop down to the bar and have a couple of halves of Guinness. After all, we were in Ireland the home of Guinness. Alex Higgins and John Virgo, the top-ranked snooker players were due in the bar where I was sitting, so I decided to stay and get acquainted.

Soon enough, I'd had one to many, and thought it best to get up to the hotel room while I was still standing. Dave was probably then fast asleep in his room thinking that I was in my room too. Something was going on around in my head. I felt that I was the ghost of my usual self. I felt lost, alone and deserted. I was having an attack from Mr. Destroyer. My entourage were around me, but I couldn't explain my feelings of loneliness and I was too proud to tell anybody. I felt that I was fighting a losing battle. I was confused.

To top it all, while trying to get some sleep, there came a knock on the door, Mark West, who was one of my cornermen, opened it and standing there were two Irish lassies. I told them to leave as I had a very important appointment the next day. Worst, Mark and I along with the other hotel guests had to be evacuated onto the cold November streets outside because we were told that the Europa hotel was about to be blown up by the IRA.

There was, simply, too much which went wrong, even before the fight.

The actual fight

Regardless of how I was feeling, losing was never an option. This was a very important fight, which could make or break my career.

The McGuigan entourage arrived for the weigh-in at the Ulster Hall. Barry was his usual rippled outstandingly fit self. There was not an ounce of fat on him. He was in fantastic shape. Barry weighed in a few grams under the featherweight limit, which is 126 pounds, or equivalent to 9 stone.

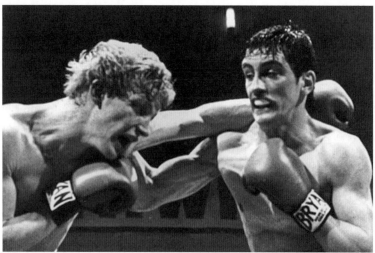

9 November 1982 at Ulster Hall, Belfast.

I, on the other hand, weighed in 3 pounds or so over the limit, which was due to having a couple of jars of Guinness the night before. So off to the boiler room we went with our skipping rope and black dustbin liners at hand. I skipped hard for an hour, then went back to the scales where I dipped in just a fraction under the nine stone limit.

Considering I'd been up half the night, I needed an urgent rest. After a good meal, I returned to 'the by now all clear' hotel room for an afternoon of undisturbed and well-deserved sleep.

In the dressing room that night, I was asked what fanfare I wanted to enter into the ring with. I chose 'Fanfare for the Common Man' by Emerson Lake and Palmer. I thought that was most fitting for the grand occasion.

I felt relaxed, as we were called to the ring. I had a good capable cornerman team around me, Frank Duffett, Dave Harris, my sparring partner Mark West and his dad and trainer, Trevor. As I was led to the ring, 'Fanfare for the Common Man' loudly whipped up the atmosphere.

Ulster Hall was alive with excitement. I climbed into the arena, raising my hands in the air. Barry's team were already in the ring. Before the fight, Barry's dad, Patrick McGuigan sang, 'Danny boy'. Patrick himself was somewhat a celebrity. He won fourth place in the Eurovision song contest back in 1968 and was a well-respected song writer too, and of course, a proud dad.

Barry 'The Clones Cyclone' McGuigan and Paul 'The Fireball' Huggins were now about to explode into a battle of the elements. The Referee called us to the centre of the ring. After his instructions for a good and fair fight, we returned to our corners and waited for the bell to sound for the first round. Cautiously, we spent most of the first-round sizing each other up. I took up my usual position with my front foot firmly lodged in place at the centre of the ring. This was the stance that I found most effective for two reasons:

First, it was a place where I could conserve energy and second, it was a place that could force my opponent onto his back foot, meaning, your opponent would have to back track and move in the wider circle, and this in turn will make him run twice the distance on the outskirts of the ring. Depending on the other man's preferred stance, this would eventually determine the outcome. More often than not, the stronger, more aggressive fighter would gain the advantage.

You have to understand that boxing involves some mental skill and analysis too.

I found out early in our fight that Barry liked to be the aggressor as much as I did, which, of course, would make for a very exiting fight.

By the third round, Barry and I had settled down to a skillful exchange of unarmed combat. We were both world class pro fighters who wanted to get to the top of the rank and become World Champions. Our exchanges which were varied were exciting the crowd into a frenzy of rapturous and very loud encouragement. From my corner, Frank was happy with the way the fight was going. He knew that by the fifth round, if fit, I could change gear again, I was capable of turning the fight towards my advantage.

The fifth round came. It was a long hard round with both fighters not giving an inch. Our punching exchanges were aggressive with a 'knock me out if you can' attitude. Barry and I were both box savvy enough to move off using our outer ring skills, throwing long stiff left jabs and left right combinations. I waited patiently for an exposure of the chin or inner rib, where, if I connected, could take my opponent out with a single shot.

The time for the end of the fifth round was approaching, I had Barry backed up into the neutral corner. The capacity audience were going wild, the noise was huge. It was awesome! The referee was looking closely to see if he would have to break the action because of holding, but so far, he'd had an easy time. It was a good, clean fight.

Sadly, our own referee was just about to change all that. Nobody heard it. The bell was ringing for the end of the fifth round. Barry and I were both unaware that the bell was ringing and carried on fighting, seconds into what now should have been our rest time. Then the ref spotted his mistake and realised that he needed to part us and direct both fighters back to our corners. He leaped and waved his arms in the air to signify that the round was over. Meanwhile, the 'McGuigan's camp' took full advantage of the moment. They all jumped into the ring, leaping up and down in the confused commotion, and, to give Barry his due, he shouted to me, *"Raise your hands in the air, Paul!"*

It appeared to me that everything was in shambles. My trainer, Frank jumped in the ring and splashed a sponge full of water over the referee.

Confused, I asked the referee: *"What are you doing?"*

He replied: *"Im sorry, Paul, I lost my bottle!"*

The decision that night did not stop Barry's bookie manager and promoter from taking my own thousand-pound bet that I had on myself to win. Fair enough, I guess. However, a few weeks after, I received a call from Barry's camp, apologizing for what had happened in the fight and offering me another go. I did not take it because I was overweight and back to my old habits of drinking and merry-making. In retrospect, perhaps the bell wasn't ringing, perhaps it was just the ref's fault.

Anyhow, I am proud of what Barry had accomplished for the sports. Barry went on to win the coveted prize of the WBA world featherweight championship title. I met him many years later at a boxing show in St. Leonards. We both got in the ring and shared a few words. Maybe I should have asked the time-keeper to ring the bell, just for old time's sake.

The Italian Job

One day I received a phone call from Dennie Mancini. He offered me a three-thousand-pound purse to fight Vincenzo Limatola in Salerno Italy.

Dennie was a well-respected man in boxing with over a decade experience in the pro game. He was a cuts man for fighters Like Richie Woodhall, Chris Eubanks, Nigel Ben and Charlie Magri.

For those who are not acquainted with boxing, a 'cuts' man is a person responsible for managing, preventing and treating the fighter's physical damage during a fight. His job is crucial for a fighter's victory in the ring. He is so important that he can decide to stop the fight, to avoid further injury or harm to a fighter.

Dennie was also a promoter, an agent and a London Soho Lonsdale boxing shop owner.

Vincenzo was both the European Boxing Union and the Italian featherweight champion, but this match was not for a title. This was supposed to be a warm up for his next title defense. Dennie's offer of three thousand ponds plus expenses, back and forth, was too enticing not to take.

The fight was only eleven days away, so I put the phone down. I finished off the almost empty bottle of Vodka and put my joint out in the ashtray. I then went and ran a cold bath, reflecting on how I would be able to get down to nine stone and four pounds, and to get fit at very short notice.

The next day with my new Hastings trainer and work boss, Peter Smith, I went to the gym with gusto. Peter loved his boxing and would do anything for the love of the sport. He gave me a job on his plastering firm as a Hod carrier for two purposes: to keep me out of trouble and, of course, cement carrying was a good job for fitness.

It helped me lose 10 pounds and make the weight for the fight. I also stuck to the fish, chicken and salad diet, with plenty of fruits, vegetables, protein shakes, natural yoghurt with wild honey.

I have a sweet tooth but I strictly refrained from sweets and anything with sugar, even butter. I willingly sacrificed alcohol and drugs.

I did the right things that a Pro boxer should be doing. I felt fit and capable leading up to this flight. I was, like a pit bull terrier, keen to be unleashed for battle.

Training hard before the fight in our headquarters above the Lord Nelson Pub.

The day before the fight, Pete, Dave and I took off from Gatwick airport, in a first-class flight en route to Leonardo da Vinci Airport in Rome. Two and a half hours later, we were greeted by a number of smartly dressed men in black Crombie coats. I didn't know if we were going to a funeral or a Mafia convention. We were led to a very nice Mercedes minibus and driven to Salerno, which was almost a 3-hour drive down towards and past Naples.

As we climbed the steep mountainous road towards our final destination, I noticed, next to the road, that there were nectarine fruit trees with lush ripe fruits hanging from their branches. I asked the driver to stop, and he gladly obliged. I was so thirsty from drying out to get down to the weight limit, I could not resist the temptation any longer.

I got out of the bus. It must have been almost midnight and 35 Celsius. I looked down toward the brightly lit bay, which had some boats moored up. The clear darkened sky was littered with twinkling stars. It was beautiful.

I picked some nectarine lush fruits from its tree, shoveling them down my parched throat with relish. Refreshed and satisfied, we resumed our journey.

We arrived at Salerno not long after midnight, where we were welcomed by a group of cheerful and friendly relieved Italians, and topped with an amazing Italian meal, which I would regret eating at weigh-in time. Unfortunately for me, the weigh-in was on that very same day scheduled for mid-day. Only ten or so hours away!

Getting on the scales, I was 4 pounds above the limit.

We went and found a vacant room that had hot running water and a bath in it. Peter handed me a skipping rope. I skipped 10 minutes as fast as I could then jumped into the hottest water that I could bare and stay there for approximately three minutes. It had worked in the past, so there was no reason why it would not work that time.

We repeated the tested method 3 times, but at the weigh in, we were told I was still over the limit. We went back for another skip and another bath.

I climbed on the scales and weighed still two ounces over the limit. I was told to do it one more time.

This time I refused outright. What little energy I had left, I wanted to save for the evening fight. The Officials then declared, that I was to forfeit some of my purse, because I refused.

"I won't do that either," followed by, *"I'm not fighting at all!"*

With that, I said to Dave and Pete, *"Let's go. We're going home!"* I picked up my training bag and headed for the exit.

Being that we were the main event that evening, the officials were left with a huge dilemma. They decided not to lose me. They hurriedly called me back and the Officials apologised for any inconvenience.

The fight was back on with no penalties.

I felt much better when Dave kindly got me a very nice, freshly made Italian ice cream. It was just what I needed. A gelato, as the Italians call it.

After all my drama, we were treated to an amazing meal by the Italians: a large white fish, which seemed to have been roasted in a wood fire oven, with sea salt, some olives, tomatoes, rice, Italian salad and, of course, pizza. All these were all washed down with red wine, presumably non-alcoholic.

Certainly, the Italians take their food seriously. Then, I napped for a few hours to refresh myself before the fight.

Show time

Show time had arrived. Vincenzo and I climbed into the ring.

We were fighting in an open-air arena in front of tens of thousands of spectators. I'd gone through the usual warm up and pep talk in our dressing room. I felt good, even pleased with myself that leading to this fight I had managed to stay away from Mr. Destroyer, if only for 11 days.

"This is it," I told myself, *"I am ready."*

I looked over at my opponent. He looked confidently composed. The TV cameras were rolling, but there was a delay. We were to be shown live on national television but to sync in with their primetime sports TV viewing time, we had to wait for approximately fifteen minutes before the battle commenced.

I used the time to unsettle my opponent. I began to show boat around the ring, just like I had seen one of my heroes, the great Cassius Clay, had done in the past. After all, I was a showman at heart, so I played to the crowd.

Pointing over at Vincenzo, I began tapping my chin then falling to the canvas, indicating what was going to happen to him. I then danced around the ring canvass wobbling and falling to my knees again, indicating Vincenzo's tragic ending to our fight.

At last, we were called to the centre of the ring. I didn't take my eyes off from his, and he knew I meant business. We were talked through the rules by the referee and then went back to our corners ready for the bell. The bell sounded for round one.

I went straight to the centre of the ring because that's where I could control the fight and save energy. Vincenzo was an upright boxer with hands which were as fast as lightning. It wasn't long into the first round that I found out that he could punch too. On my front foot approach, Vincenzo caught me with a left right counter combination, both hitting me flush on my face, the right cross almost popping my eye out.

I stepped back and could feel my left eye closing up. I needed both eyes with this man. I was beginning to see double. I shook my head, vigorously. Thankfully, my vision returned but I had to recover very, very quickly or I would lose it in the first round.

As I stepped back, Vincenzo came at me like a lion. Because he had spotted that I was in trouble, he came in for the kill, but I was ready. I leaned back and caught my man with a clean right cross to his jaw. I saw for a split second that he wobbled. It was a good shot and like a red flag to a bull, I ripped into Vincenzo with all I could muster from the souls of my feet upwards. I felt the power surging through my legs as I laid into my opponent with crashing left right-left combinations. My body punching was lethal, I could take an opponent out with a single blow. I hit him with all I had. The referee stepped in to give Vincenzo a standing count.

The referee waved us both back into battle. I steamed at my man like a locomotive, and there was no stopping me now. My adrenalin was pumping. I knew this could be my night. I could show once again that I could be a World Champion contender.

After 2 minutes, 36 seconds of the first round, the referee jumped in to save Vincenzo Limatola from any further punishment. The fight was mine.

This time, I was the one who roared at the screaming crowd like a lion, which didn't go down too well. The crowd proceeded to pick up the chairs and began throwing them into the ring.

Peter jumped into the ring to protect me, and while covering me, shouted, *"Paul, they are trying to kill us!"* Peter then told me, *"Go over to Vincenzo and put his hand in the air."*

I did. Then I tried to calm the crowd by praising Vincenzo and clapping for him. By this time, the armed police had surrounded the ring. We were safe.

Back in Hastings, my victory was announced in the papers. The Hastings Observer's Sports headline read, 'The Fireball does the Italian Job'.

I was very pleased with myself and, for countless times, promised my Manager and Trainers that I would try harder.

During this fight, I was placed in the British Boxing Board of Controls rankings at number one in the UK, number five in Europe and number ten in the world.

Not bad for a Hastings boy with so much potential but who blew it because he lacked the sense to keep himself out of trouble, addictions, and all the other temptations he could not resist from Mr. Destroyer.

My last fight

I fought The European Champion, Jean Marc Renard, in Belgium on Christmas day 1987 for my last fight.

For this fight, I was trained by Bob Paget.

Bob was a lovely man who was the founder member of the kids' charity 'Angels with Dirty Faces.' Bob's motto was, 'Do someone a good turn and don't tell anyone about it'.

Bob was the type of man who sees the good in everyone.

Heading for Bruges in Belgium, Bob and my good friend from Hastings, Keith, who I chose to be my other corner man, got on the ferry at Newhaven Ferry Port. We were heading for Bruges in Belgium where Jean Marc Renard lived.

Boxing had taken me to beautiful places, both in the UK and other parts of Europe, but not being on a holiday, I failed to take in the views and appreciate what was before me.

Bruges is a beautiful city with picturesque cobbled streets and canals, churches, towers, castles, bridges, and many other historic buildings, which dated back to the mid-fifteen hundreds. As we wandered around, I could not help but notice that it is best to see it 'on foot'. It looked like you were in a fairy tale land.

Anyways, I am glad that I appreciated Bruges, because the fight did not go well in my favour. To be honest, all I wanted at this stage in my boxing career was the money. I was nearly in my thirties, and had somehow slowly lost the motivation to prove that I was still a good fighter. I was busy pursuing the senseless pleasures of life and severely lacked the sense to keep fit and train consistently. It was just a matter of time before I threw in the towel.

Bob aptly described me as 'mental'.

In any sport, both mental and physical fitness are indispensable for victory.

Giving all I got nonetheless, I managed to stay in the fight until the eighth round. And then I hit the wall, as if every ounce of my strength was drained out of me. I could hardly hold my hands up, as if to signal surrendering. I became totally defenseless, which meant vulnerable and open to everything that Jean wanted to fire at me. Bob had no other choice but to throw the towel in before my pride killed me. It was all over. Jean was the man of the match.

That night, Bob, Keith and I drowned our sorrows in the bar.

In the morning, Keith and I decided to get on a train and pop down to Amsterdam for a few days.

I shook Bob's hand and thanked him for his kindness and having a Christmas day with me rather than his family. I also told him, "I would come and find him to collect my purse when I ran out of money." I did, three months later.

Once Keith and I had got down to the Dam by train, I felt better. Keith and I did what most people would normally do in Amsterdam. For example, visit the 'weed' coffee shops, patronise the sex trade, visit the Van Gogh art museum and take the cruise in the sightseeing barges.

For me, Amsterdam was a place of freedom and adventure, but a long weekend was usually more than enough. No matter how much fun our holidays are, we often long for the familiar, for normality, for our home.

As you will find out, later, after I retired from professional boxing, Amsterdam, would become a hub for me for my cannabis drugs smuggling operation to Hastings.

And so, with this fight, my boxing career ended.

Throughout my professional career, I was privileged to have been trained and managed by some of the best such as Dave Harris, Barret and Duff Promotions, Frank Duffett, Bob Paget, and Frank Warren, but unfortunately, I was the Champion that never really was.

If only I knew what I know, now, who knows what I could have achieved in the game I love!

PART 2:

_____

DRUG DEALING,
CHARITY EVENTS,
DEATH ENCOUNTERS,
THAILAND, PRISON.

The beginning of my drug trading and smuggling operations with the cartel

Had I taken note of the proverbial saying, 'make hay when the sun is shining', I would have saved enough money to tide me over until my retirement.

But obviously, I simply had no sense. Paraphrasing George Best, I spent most of my money on wine, women, and song, and the rest I squandered.

I began to look for other ways to earn a living and what seemed attractive and easy money was the drug trafficking cartel.

Since I was very well known around town, it didn't take long to find out how it all worked. I found out who was doing what and where. It was a whole new ball game. I didn't think or care about the potential consequences of my actions, nor the harm that drugs caused.

The fact that I would be getting all my own drugs free, was an added incentive. All I had to do was go to the street dealers' homes and tell them that I would supply them with a weekly amount of cannabis on a 'pay when sold' arrangement.

It wasn't long before I had numerous clienteles and ruthlessly involved in a drug smuggling and trading cartel. We smuggled drugs from Amsterdam and, of course, got them from big local cartels.

If I were to compare myself to what I was in the criminal gravy chain to a piece on a chess board, I would probably say a knight.

I was always weaving around trying to avoid trouble while finding a way to check mate over the winning line.

The drug trade can get very messy. There were a number of occasions when I had to go with an accomplice to certain addresses armed with a hammer or a piece of 4 by 2 wood and literally smash the door in to demand my money. I also carried a jungle machete hidden in the boot of my car.

If the debt wasn't paid after a week or two, I would personally take great pleasure in hurting whosoever had ripped me off my money.

There was no honour amongst thieves. Too many times, you could get ripped off at the drop of a hat by an out-of-towner. I lost thousands of pounds of dirty money from fellow criminals. Even your very own drug fence would rip you off, along with elaborate stories.

In a reasonably small town like Hastings, especially then in the late 80s till the 90s, when people were very much acquainted with everyone's business, I had to be careful not to arouse the suspicion of the police.

I came up with a clever plan to divert the police's attention from my relatively extravagant lifestyle. Oh well, it was not really that clever, but the oldest trick in the book for criminals, along with money laundering, which was to operate a legitimate business.

I had a keen interest in the collection of pre-war antiquities, and a firm believer that 'one man's rubbish is another man's riches, so I decided to establish a buy and sell business of antiques. My old friend Steve and I bought a good second-hand transit van and had it spray painted into a nice medium brown colour, with cream old-English wording, with the name, 'Antique-a-Brac'. We took the van all over the south of England, buying and selling old stuff. You would find us everywhere in auction sites and boot fairs. We even had our own indoor stall at St. Leonards.

While life seemed to be smooth sailing for me, despite my hidden drug related activities, it would not last long, as you will discover later. The old adage, 'crime does not pay', is so very true for most of us, either here on earth, or the life beyond in hell.

All it ever did to me, essentially, was what Mr. Destroyer intended it to do, DESTROY my life. I wish that it was limited to my life but it also caused havoc in my family, loved ones and four good friends. The latter all perished in sudden, untimely deaths.

One was a prolific sportsman, who had so much talent. Drugs turned him into a shadow of his former self. One day, without warning, he sat in his bath and shot himself through the head. Another friend, a very good boxer with a beautiful family, was found hanging in the kitchen by his wife. Two other friends, as I will write about later, tragically lost their lives to drugs as well.

Meanwhile, I had to carry on pretending, even to myself, that I was living a normal life.

And being a Jekyll and Hyde, I was also involved in some good causes.

Charity events

Hastings is a tourist destination, especially during summer months, which meant the town had to offer lots of activities; town carnival fairs, beach parties, seafood festivals, music festivals, summer town fairs, to name a few.

As I have previously mentioned, the most popular one was the Old Town carnival week in the month of August.

In the early 90s, my fisherman friend David Kirly and I decided to raise money for the Hastings Hospice Foundation. The idea was to build a boxing ring in the centre of Winkle Island, from where, like what they did in the old times, I would take on all comers, or those who wanted to try boxing with me.

Days before the event, we printed yellow T-shirts with the Foundation's name on the back, but we still did not have a ring.

It wasn't long before we had a ring all set up and ready to go. Hastings has always had a sense of community where people just help each other.

We spotted Bob, who owned a scaffolding company. After explaining what our intentions were, the three of us went to Bob's lorry and hauled off eight of the longest scaffold tubes we could find with four short corner posts. David went over to the beach to his shed and found some old sailing canvas, some strings and some old cushions, which we used for the corner posts.

All we needed now was someone who could be our referee. Then I remembered Danny Stupple, who was an ex-Pro boxing Master of Ceremonies Official back in the day. Conveniently, Danny was also the landlord of the Royal Standard Pub opposite Winkle Island, the venue. I went and asked if he would join in with the frolics, which he did, willingly. Tracey Shipley, the landlady of the Nelson Pub, had a spare megaphone and a couple of pairs of boxing gloves and two head guards were borrowed from up at the Old Town Tackleway Boxing Club.

Around mid-day, on the day of the event, there was a bit of a crowd gathering at Winkle Island. Danny began to announce what we were doing and for whom we were doing it. It wasn't long before I had my first volunteer opponent, brave enough to get in the ring with me. That's all that was needed.

After the first, everybody wanted to get in. There were girls, boys, men, women, all getting in one at a time, one after the other.

All afternoon, the ring was surrounded with cheering and laughing, from all sorts of folks.

It was all fun except for one lad, who didn't want to play like all the others. He got a little serious trying to beat me up. I had to give him a swift left hook on the jaw, which put him on his backside. I helped him back up.

We raised a fair amount of cash that day. The local Hospice was very pleased with us.

With all good intentions, we repeated it as long as we could. One event, we matched up some of the Old Town fishermen with each other.

Understandably, it did not sit well with the Hastings Borough Council. They called it 'an organised, grievous bodily harm event'.

In reality it was 'sorting the men out from the boys'.

To us it was just a bit of fun. No harm really intended and all for a good cause.

Another time on Carnival Day, I joined a grand procession in my Old Austin England A 35. It was one of the later models produced in the 1950s and early 60s. A lovely old car. It was a good excuse for me to dress up. I borrowed a kid's paddling pool to tie onto the roof so people could throw money in it.

I wore a nice black suit and trilby hat. I blackened my face up with pantomime paint, put a pair of white gloves on, then joined in the show. I loved to show my little Austin off, especially for charity, but this time, I had made the mistake of putting the paddling pool on the top.

On our way round, in the colorful procession, I found myself wincing every time I heard a coin hit the roof.

And there, my poor car took the beating, again all for a good cause.

CHAPTER 18

Escape to Thailand

By my early thirties, I'd had numerous failed relationships with wonderful women. I blamed all the failures on myself. The drinks and the drugs were far more important to me. When I was sober and focused, I could be a respectable young man who would do anything to help anyone but the easy money from criminal activities was also too powerful for me to break free from.

One relationship I had, I sired 3 beautiful children. When my first son was born, I was so wickedly selfish that I was with my dog, Lucy, drinking in a pub. I did not care at all.

It was an on and off relationship and she never deserved how I treated her. Still, one day, I decided to make true my promise to change. I went to her nice, cozy flat hoping for a fresh start. I brought flowers, fruits and some goodies for the children. I knocked and no one answered. I realised that the door was unlocked, opened it and let myself in. Only to find out that the whole flat was empty. There was nothing there but a little hamster running around, free from its cage. They had left.

I could not blame them. She was free at last. The picture which went through my mind was that she finally found the courage to escape from me and our bad, drunken, drugged and violent relationship."

They were gone, for good, perhaps. And I was devastated.

Too devastated, that the next day, I went down to a travel agent to escape my reality, and to try to escape the monster who I had become.

I'd recently seen a programme on the telly which showed Thailand.

Even during those times, in the early 90s, it looked like a great holiday destination. It showed lots of beautiful women and the nightlife culture looked like from another world.

I booked a 3-month open ticket to Bangkok, where I thought I could find myself and where I was going in life. I thought it could be a place where I could forget all my troubles.

I would soon find out that it did not disappoint.

Before I left, I told my associates in my drug trade to get on with our business and that I would be back after 2 to 3 months. I packed a small rucksack with the bare necessities.

After our stop off at Muscat, we proceeded to Bangkok International Airport.

I've never been too keen on flying, especially the landing stage. Usually, when landing, I cling on for dear life. Apparently, there are more chances of being struck by lightning than having a plane crash.

Anyways, I was almost refused entry, because I got a little drunk from the booze on board our flight. The Customs demanded to see my passport and how much money I had. I showed them my traveler's cheques along with my British cash and passport. They were then satisfied that I would be spending plenty of money in their country. So, they let me through to the arrival lounge.

I hailed a taxi on to my next adventure. My first in an Asian country.

My first night in Bangkok

The big man insisted on carrying my rucksack to the awaiting car. My driver, whose name was Samoi, seemed like a friendly man. He spoke pretty good English. He even took me around to show me a little of the neighborhood 'at no extra cost'! We eventually found a reasonably priced hotel room that had an air-con. I asked Samoi if he would come and get me the very next morning, mainly because he had treated me so well. He agreed to be at the hotel before 10 am. I paid him and gave him a nice tip. I had made a friend.

Bangkok night life area covers many square miles. If I were to compare it, it is the size of central London. Like a child who just stepped inside a fantasy park, I unpacked my bag, had a shower, put on my glad rags and decided to investigate if what I saw on the telly was true. On the way down to the busy street, I took one last look at the hotel I was staying in.

A three-wheeled contraption, which is called a 'tuk-tuk', pulled up beside me and asked if I needed a ride. Before long, we were in the City Centre.

Looking around me, I was amazed at what I saw. There were bars everywhere, of all shapes and sizes, carts being pushed around with piles of goods to sell; food trolleys with deliciously smelling aromas drifting here and there and on it all went. It was all very colourful.

There was still light, so I decided to walk around. I could hardly take it all in. All the colourful characters, of different shapes and sizes, of the street traders and the beautiful women offering themselves were all remarkably interesting.

It wasn't long before I found myself in a poll dancing venue, where women danced naked. I sat at the bar and ordered a cold beer. Any beer would do. Women were coming up to me encouraging me to drink more.

As the night progressed, I kept telling myself that this was going to be a very interesting 3-month vacation. England and its woes would all be a thing of the past.

By midnight, I had had enough and was too exhausted from the flight, so I decided to call it a day. I flagged down a tuk-tuk but there was just one very important detail that I missed. I did not know the name of the hotel I was staying in. In my keen excitement to experience my first night out in Bangkok, I did not even bother to take note of the name of my hotel nor take a hotel card in my pocket.

The tuk-tuk driver could hardly speak English. In fact, he could hardly speak at all due to a bottle of whiskey that he was drinking which was concealed down between his knees.

"Where do you want to go?" my new friend asked as he passed me the bottle. I took a swig because this may very well be my last day here in Thailand.

"Just drive please," I slowly repeated about four times. *"I need to find my hotel,"* I indicated in pigeon English with anxious dread.

The skinny laughing man then took off. As we drove around the area, it seemed like we were getting nowhere. He kept taking me to various brothels and strip bars.

"No! No! No!" I had to keep repeating. *"We must find my hotel,"* I slowly exclaimed again, and again, with sign language and in almost desperate panic.

He eventually got the message. He was as determined as I was to find our elusive hotel, even if we had to go to the many hundreds of hotels in Bangkok. It was looking that way. Either that or next stop, 'The British Embassy'.

On and on we went until the early hours of the morning; zig-zagging across here, there and everywhere. By now, the morning light had begun to break into the darkness.

The thoughts that were going through my mind were, *"How ridiculous! If anyone found out that I got lost on my first day and had to come home, I could never live this down. I'd be the laughing stock. I would have to make up a story of why I had arrived back home so soon."*

But then, just before losing all hope, there, as we went round a bend, I saw it. I saw my hotel.

I can tell you; I was the happiest man on the planet at that moment. I gave the tuk-tuk driver a handsome fare, which was a week's wages by their standards. Thanking the Tuk Tuk laughing man and with great relief, I had time to have a couple of hours rest before Samoi turned up.

My second day and the kickboxing

I soon woke up to the sound of the phone tinkling in my ear and it turned out to be Samoi. We came to an agreement that I would pay Samoi a daily wage until further notice. He would be my driver.

That day, we drove to many tourist destinations: The Golden Buddha, the many temples of the Golden Buddha, the elephant show, the river traders and then to a nice Thai restaurant.

The next day, Samoi took me to a kickboxing stadium. The place was packed. I noticed that before the fight every fighter went through a spiritual dance routine, adorned with colourful head dress, and with music. The music sounded much like it came from a snake charmer. This was all performed before each fight. During the fights, loud cries would go up whenever a fighter kicked and punched, and landed scoring blows on their opponents. Almost everyone in the arena was waving their hands in the air, holding money.

I noticed bookie-type men who were spotted here there and everywhere. They were taking bets, waving their hands to and fro, drawing attention to each other, and they were using special sign language. It looked like you could bet at any time during the fight. Even up till the very last seconds of the final bell. It was all very impressive.

Then he took me to the zoo, which I was not really very impressed with because the animals were crammed in cages and I thought the RSPCA would have a handful to rescue and deal with this lot.

Of course, I was enjoying the night life, but you can have too much of a good thing. I asked Samoi how life was like for the people who lived in the mountains and what they did for a living.

He told me that his family worked and lived up in the mountains. Then he asked me if I'd like to visit his family with him.

Delighted, I said," *Yes, that would be greatly appreciated.*"

So, with that, we arranged to meet the next morning for our journey up into the mountains.

I was thrilled. The change of scenery would be as good as a rest.

A family outing and my life up in the mountains

Samoi turned up to my hotel the next morning with his wife and kids. I then checked out.

The 4 hour or so drive for me was an adventure in itself.

We passed by the paddy fields, the coconut and banana plantations and water melon fields. There were vast lakes, which Samoi said were filled with fresh water fish and prawns. They, too, were taken care of by the farming communities.

The various birds' species were also to me a sight to behold. The mountains in the distance stretched up and above the clouds. It was all so much more serene and a far cry from the hustle and bustle of the city that we had left behind.

Time soon past us by until we were off of the main roads and on to the dusty tracts heading towards Samoi's home village.

As we arrived in the village, we were greeted by Samoi's friends and in-laws. The families lived in a number of wooded houses that were constructed on top of sturdy 3 metre or so wooden legs. This I learned was practical for two reasons, to stop the tigers from coming in for a human meal and for storage space. The houses had thatched roofs.

There were chicken's hutches that housed the loose roaming chickens. They laid fresh eggs for the early morning collection.

There were tools, hammocks and all sorts of stuff for their farm work. Outside the entrance of each house was a foot bath, which everybody used before entering. The family house that I was lodging in had polished dark-wood floorboards. There were 4 built-in wooden beds each with a straw-filled mattress and all with mosquito nets. The toilet was a box cubical that had a hole in the wooden floor, where your doo-doos fell down into a cesspit. The water supply for cooking and washing was pumped up from a well in the ground. The cooking stove was a genius type of contraption made of clay, that had a metal mesh on which the food was placed to cook over the embers, somewhat like a barbecue. The place for food preparation was squeezed in under the wooden house along with the pots and pans. If lighting was needed, there was a petrol generator which would only be used if and when necessary.

When the families needed supplies other than food, they would go into town 15 or so miles away in their old beaten-up diesel trucks.

That night after all the formalities of the day in broken English, I was shown to my bed that belonged to one of the family members. They'd given it up for me and found somewhere else to sleep. Samio stayed for a couple of days, but needed to get back to work with his family. He said he would come and get me in three weeks.

Nobody could speak much English, but we managed to communicate with lots of smiles and sign language. The people in Samio's village all treated me very well. They were very generous too with what they had.

Throughout the day we would eat amazing food, fresh laid eggs, corn on the cobs, all types of fresh water fish and prawns, pork, beef, clay oven baked breads, vegetables and fruits of various kinds. Everything was unbelievably scrumptious, except I always preferred to have mine with less chilli.

Work for the men and woman would start from very early in the morning at dawn. Coconut trucks would turn up and take people away to work in the paddy fields and other plantations. The kids would go to the village school later in the morning and when they had finished, we would play football and swim in the river.

It was a wonderfully serene and simple way of life, but not necessarily devoid of debauchery.

At night, I would go with the older boys to other village huts where we would smoke strong skunkweed and drink whiskey called 'lao khao', which was 100% proof, pure alcohol made from rice. The weed and booze when combined were lethal. I was always being warned not to wander off, as I was prone to do while under the influence. I was told that I could well be killed by wild animals like the roaming tigers or even strangers from other village tribes.

One day, I was taken by car up into the mountains. The boys had a skunkweed plantation there. When we eventually arrived, I could smell the distinctive aroma wafting through the 34c or so light midday breeze. Two of the boys left to collect a certain amount from the Skunk bushes which weren't so far away. I was left with one of the other lads. When the others got back, our driver turned to me and said, *"This is where you die."* I made a joke of it.

Thankfully, he was joking too. I think he meant I would die if I ever told anybody about their big secret. Their small, but effective, operation was constant, because in that sort of climate the skunk weed never stops growing. Selling small amounts in packets to the tourists gave them an ongoing flow of income.

Back at the village, it was time for an all-important meal.

I was lounging on a hammock under the house when one of the boys brought along, from a nearby field, a medium sized cow. What followed was a first for me.

The cow was taken to the back of where we lived and tied to a post. The boy then went to fetch a sharp knife, while other villagers came and gathered round the cow, chanting. This was going to be ours and half of the village's meal for the next two or three weeks.

Before the boy cut the cow's throat, to soften the pain, I felt the need to make the animal dazed, so I picked up a sledge hammer from beneath the house and hit the cow over the head with it. The animal fell to its knees. Then the knife was drawn swiftly across its throat. A bowl collected the blood.

Soon the animal stopped its twitching and then the highly professional dissecting began. Nothing was wasted, even the hoofs would be carved to make trinkets to sell to the tourists. We ate well that night and in the days that followed.

All very delicious too

My last week came, and thankfully, because I was missing the night life.

Before my departure, the boys showed me a brochure on Koh Samui Island, a beautiful paradise, which was to be my next destination.

The day soon came when Samoi arrived at the village to pick me up. We said our goodbyes with lots of shaking hands and hugging.

I then checked out Koh Samui Island, where I spent a few days with fellow backpackers. Koh Samui is the second largest island in Thailand with white sand beaches.

It looked like paradise but time flies when you are having fun. Before long, my vacation was nearing its end.

The last week at Thailand: Snooker and Boxing

During my last week at Thailand, I discovered a snooker hall.

We were playing for good hard cash. I thought that I was good, but the man I was playing against was proving to be much better than me. He had a crafty game plan. He was playing me like a fiddle to make the game seem very close. Then dynamically, he would skillfully knock in the last few balls to clinch the game and the money. He beat me three games on the trot.

I thought I'd better quit or I'll be skinned.

I noticed that there were many framed pictures of fighting men hanging on the snooker hall walls. I said to my hustling friend that I'd had enough of snooker and perhaps we can have a nice wager with me fighting one of these guys up on the wall. My snooker opponent was not surprised.

Apparently, I had managed to acquire a nick-name already. They called me *'The Mad Farang'*, which meant mad European white man.

He called one of his gang member friends over. They spoke a few words in Thai, and then started laughing.

"You waun figh?" asked the well-dressed colourful character of medium build. He was smiling at me. I noticed he had a front gold tooth, so I smiled back because I have two gold teeth, too.

"You waun figh?" he asked again.

I nodded, *"Yes, I want to fight."*

"You cum whi me," said Glitter Lips.

I was led to the back of the hall. We went to a door that had 'Gym Personnel Only' written on it. I was ushered in. It was a gym with cubicles with a bed in each one where the fighters slept. It was a reasonable size boxing gym with punch bags and all the usual boxing gear, skipping ropes, speed balls etc., but no boxing ring.

What struck me was that there were ropes tied to the wooden beams above that hung down to the floor. Young strong, very fit looking men were climbing up and down the ropes using just their hands and arms. They were climbing all the way to the top, and then slowly back down again.

I had never seen this technique in boxing training before. It was impressive. They were all very fit lads. I could see there were a number of other rooms with beds in them. Obviously, these fighters were being looked after and used by the triad gangs, much like cockerel fighting, but with humans.

"*You chwes who you wauna figh,*" repeated Mr Glitter Lips, twice.

I looked around. I was spoilt for choice. They were all in great shape.

I, on the other hand, was a little flabby. I'd been out on the town far too long to go the distance. I carefully looked round the room, eyeing every one up.

I pointed to a lad in his late teens, "*That one,*" I said confidently. I might not be as fit as him, but I know I had far more experience.

"*So, what was next?*" I wondered. I soon found out.

"*Forrow us,*" said Glitter Lips.

The gym looked to me to be practically used more of less for sparing purposes only. There were a few pairs of gloves hanging up and a large mirror for shadow boxing screwed to the wall. There was an open cubical room with buckets of water in them which were used for washing yourself down. It wasn't impressive.

This was going be a brutal and raw war. The rules were decided. We would fight with gloves on. Three-minute rounds with a 1-minute rest period. No kicking or biting.

Winner would be declared when the other had had enough. In other words, we were fighting to the death.

I put all the money I had left on me that night to win.

Glitter lips matched my bet, which Mr. Hustler held to award to the winner.

He was smiling like a Cheshire cat.

The war begins

Set and ready, the bell sounded for the first round.

I did my normal thing and settled straight away into the centre of the relatively small ring. You couldn't run and hide in here. The lad was fit and sharp. I tried to cut his moving space off as best I could, throwing my own jabs with left right combinations. He was strong too, as he held his ground and hit me back with some good, solid counter punches. I pushed forward as a prowler would, and I found myself covering up more than I threw punches as he was coming at me with everything he had. The bell sounded for rest time. It seemed to me like a very long round.

I looked at my man and noticed that he hadn't yet broken into a sweat, and he was breathing with ease. I, on the other hand was puffing away like an old man who had just climbed up a tower block of stairs. I had nobody in my corner to give me some encouraging advice.

But I did not really need any advice. At that point, I needed an oxygen mask. *'Ding, ding,'* and back we went for the next round.

My opponent was even stronger in the second round. He caught me with a cracking right full on my jaw. I was glad to have found an old gum shield to use before the battle commenced, as I fear old glitter lips would be retrieving my teeth from the warn canvass decking. I struggled through the round as best I could. At last, the bell rang which ended the second round. Again, it seemed the 3 minutes took forever to end.

I went to my corner wheezing out and sucking in the 34c night air. There was no air! There was no stall either, so I slumped down and sat on the canvass ring floor. The bell sounded far too soon for the third round. I barely climbed to my feet. This was turning into a nightmare. It seemed like my man could sense defeat. He tore at me like a bull. I tucked in, covering up as best I could, and hit back at my opponent's body with as much strength as I could muster. By now, my tongue was bleeding and a mouse was beginning to swell on my right eye. The bell for the end of the third round didn't come too soon.

I staggered back to my lonely corner with blood trickling from my mouth. I went over and looked in the mirror. I was marked up and wondered if my second wind would ever come. I needed oxygen badly. I began to suck in deep breaths of air.

The fourth-round bell rang. Smoking the weed and drinking too much whisky had got the better of me, and this could be my downfall. All I could do was fight from instinct. Thankfully I was still able to draw strength from somewhere.

"Let's try a new tactic," I thought to myself. It dawned on me that my past best performances were due to body punches which if landed correctly would render a man helpless. So, I dug as deep as I could, slipped under my opponents left lead then crashed a straight right cross to his soft lower rib. At that precise point there's no muscle to protect the lung. I heard a crack, and at the same time all the oxygen that my game opponent had in him drained from him as he dropped in a heap to the canvass. I tried to hit him while he was going down, but missed.

Going back to my corner, I let glitter lips take up the count. They counted up to and past thirty seconds. He did get back on his feet eventually, but then his wily crew rang the bell.

I complained, but what I got back, in broken English was, *"Yew in awe kuntry now..we mak rules…you say wan figh to deff."*

What could I do? But fight to death.

With that, after the bell, I tore into the lad and smashed the living day lights out of his body until he fell to his knees, shaking his head. He was beaten.

The bet was honoured. I took my money from the by now not so smiling Mr. Hustler. I went and shook my hurting opponent's hand. On parting, glitter lips said, *"We se yu agayn tomowo, same time."*

I politely declined, but thanked them kindly and left.

I felt good. It was time to party. I had enough money now to see me through until I got back home.

All in all, my three months stay in Thailand was a good traveler's experience, worthy of some pages here in the book.

Almost everything was entirely and relatively a new experience for me. I made some friends and was a recipient of undeserved, genuine kindness of the entire village. More importantly, since I was not a Christian, yet, and was under the illusion that I could do everything on my own, on my own terms and strength, I realised that I was able to hold my own.

Two years later, I went back to the very same snooker hall with my friend, John. Glitter Lips was still there. They recognised me immediately, and told me that my boxing friend had to take a break from the ring until his broken rib had mended.

John proved to be better at the game than me. John won our bet that night, and there was no fighting for me this time round.

Little did I know back then, that John, 'my good buddy', wouldn't be with us for much longer.

Earlier, I wrote about the tragedies of untimely deaths of my two friends due to drug dealing, and it claimed two more of my friends' lives.

CHAPTER 19

Deaths of friends and strange encounters

Every year in the town of Glastonbury near Pilton, Somerset, almost two hundred thousand people from all walks of life and from all corners of the globe travel to the Glastonbury festival for five days of performing arts. The festival is always filled with contemporary music, comedy, theatre, circus, cabaret, and other arts. Leading pop and rock artists make their appearances. Films and albums recorded at Glastonbury have been released, and the festival receives extensive television and newspaper coverage. Glastonbury is the largest green field festival in the world. And it began its simple roots back in 1970 with just a little gathering in a field, a little gathering with some big ideas, which, led to what it is today. The festival takes you through the June 21st summer solstice.

I'd been to Glastonbury before by coach, but this year, 1994, John thought it was a good idea to drive us down instead of getting the bus. We would save time and have more privacy. We had to take two cars that day. Early in the morning, we filled our cars with goodies, which included plenty of beer, weed, a map and a couple of tents. Excited and prepared, off we went on our 189 miles trip. The journey normally takes just over three and a half hours, but it would take almost five hours if you get lost, like we did.

Thankfully we managed to get there. We were all being spoilt for entertainment choices, but then, sadly, as quick as we had come, it was almost time to leave. John insisted that he had to go the day before the end. He needed to do a deal back in Hastings.

I tried as best I could to prevent him from leaving that night. I said the deal would still be there for another day, but John was having none of it. He said it was very important and worth big money. So, we said our farewells, but I knew I'd see him for a good game of golf in a day or two. John was a fine golfer because his dad taught him well.

The very next day, we ourselves had arrived back home in the early evening hours by coach. I decided to go and have a pint down at the local. It was there in the Nelly that I was told the horrible news. I couldn't believe it. It must be a mistake as I was only talking with John yesterday

John had fallen asleep tragically at the wheel of his car not far from Glastonbury. John had veered off the edge of the M3 motorway, and then careered through the perimeter fence.

I couldn't control my emotions. I cried for a whole week.

Busted

We'd all been over to Amsterdam together. We'd slept in the same rooms and been to the same bars. This other friend had cleverly devised a way of smuggling Moroccan cannabis resin through the customs. Month in, month out we were having deliveries in cases of soft drinks that Barry would personally oversee as they went through the seaport customs. It could only get better, so we thought. But then tragedy struck. One night, the police were chasing a car thief who was running from the car he had to abandon.

Sadly, for my friend, the runner ran into a seaside hotel and then into his room, followed by the police. My friend was in the room, and in possession of the contraband. He was caught red handed and taken away. He was locked up in jail until the case went to Crown court. It was yet another tragedy.

Two months later, my friend was found hanging by his neck in a London prison cell.

Disaster in the Mediterranean

Even on holidays, disaster followed me and my friends.

During the mid-90s, it was affordable to go to the Mediterranean Islands such as Greece, Malta or Tenerife. So, four of my friends decided to go to Tenerife one summer.

We were sure that we: Eddy, John, Keith and Dave, would have a grand time. Arriving at the hotel, we were a little disappointed because we were going to have to be split up into two separate parts of the hotel.

That was fine, we decided. *"Let's not let it spoil our holiday."*

Our luggage did finally turn up, only to find that one of the lad's cases had mistakenly found its way onto a flight bound for Africa.

We enjoyed our first night together.

The next day, before our outing, rather than leave my holiday money in the hotel room where it could get stolen, I thought it safer if I kept the money in the zip pocket of my shorts. We then met in the lounge and had a lovely breakfast and planned our day out. Then off we went to visit the sites. The sites in Tenerife were bar after bar after bar.

By the time midday had arrived, I had somehow wandered off and was totally lost and out of my little mind.

All I can remember that day after breakfast was being led over to a deserted place by some friendly Spaniards, who turned out to be not so friendly. I got bashed over the head and robbed of everything I had on me. I woke up disoriented. I didn't know what day of the week it was, or where I was. I had the biggest hangover I had ever had.

When I eventually came to my senses and found our hotel, there was both laughing and sympathy from my friends. I said I didn't feel well to go out that night.

That night I sat in and watched a bit of telly, feeling sorry for myself and thinking, *"Surely, this couldn't get any worse, could it?'"*

Well, it was just about to. It was a little past midnight. The door burst opened and in came John, raving about, *"There was a fight in the bar and Eddy was taken to the hospital."*

I leaped out of bed and we made our way to the emergency department. It was all a living nightmare. Eddy had a knife wound in his leg which needed a lot of stitches. We spent the next week and a half looking after Eddy. There was nothing we could do except stay sober and find out where the people responsible were.

If ever there had been a first prize for a 'clowns outing on vacation', we would have won it.

The moral of the story is, 'Never do anything foolish in a foreign country'.

In contrast, I had one of the most amazing holidays in the other part of the Mediterranean, Istanbul in Turkey, with my very good friend, an excellent mechanic, Mick Hamer. There was not much fooling around, and I was truly mesmerised, not just by the stunning sights, which I fell in love with, but by all the *'kebabs and shawarma'* in abundant quantity and quality.

It is no wonder that in this country we are drawn to kebabs too.

A strange encounter

Some nights, I and my drug associates in our little cartel would sit around each other's houses, playing music and chilling. If we ran out of smoke, there were plenty of places we could go for it.

Yet there were times, without warning, that the cannabis would go completely dry. The whole town would have none.

Shipments do not arrive, because of information leaks, and undercover surveillance was active. When this happens, shippers had no choice but to change tactics and direction.

Vigilance was always necessary and the suppliers were constantly on their toes trying to think up new ways of evading the law. At times, we were left with no choice but to stop briefly.

My friend said he knew a place where he could get some Lebanese black, which is a sticky oily black substance, and was smoked in joints or from a water bong. Personally, I didn't much care what it was. To me, drugs were all the same. Drugs were drugs, for which I had an addiction.

And so, to satisfy our cravings, the four of us got in my van and drove down to the promenade on the Hastings sea front. My friend said he wouldn't be long, and then disappeared into a block of houses.

Five or so minutes went by without a word between those of us left in the van. Just then, I was startled by a loud bang on the side of the van.

I turned to the two at the back of the van and asked, *"What's that?"*

"I dunno," replied my friends.

"OK," I said, and turned round. Then three seconds went by and another bang. I turned back again, and said, *"Don't muck about, who's that?"*

"It's not us," my friends, insisted.

I opened the van door and walked round the van. I got back in and asked the lads to sit in the middle of the van with their hands so that I could see them.

"OK, I said, to the mystery invisible man, bang on the van whoever you are."

Almost immediately, there were three successive bangs on the side of the van. *"Did you hear that!?"* I shouted.

"What on earth was that?"

I wasn't a religious man, but that strange encounter caused me to run over to the seashore to where I began splashing sea water all over my face. I thought something entered me, which gave me some supernatural knowledge and wisdom. In fact, I couldn't stop talking about what had happened for three whole days.

Strange as it was, I was very excited. I thought a spirit had entered me but as quick as it did, it quickly vanished, too. So, I assumed it did.

I was so curious about the strange encounter that I even went to a spiritualist church in Robertson Street to find out what exactly I had encountered.

The notice outside said that they would be open the next day, and so I made sure that I was there that evening.

Going in, there was a man on the door. He was nicely dressed in a black suit and tie. Surprised, I teased him, *"Did anyone die?"*

The pale gentleman smiled and said, *"You've come to the right place for that, Sir."*

"Umm, perhaps you can help me then." I was enthusiastic. I told him the story and then I asked him if he might be able to call my friendly spirit back?

"Come in," answered the odd gentleman, *"Let's see what we can do."*

With that, he took me through a door with a black curtain hanging from it and led me into a dimly lit room, which was full of people. He then politely showed me to my seat.

The man then went around lighting candles and switched off the dim lighting. A man and woman also dressed in black were standing at the front, behind a wooded altar. I presumed they were the service leaders. They began to talk and welcome everybody and inquired if there were any newcomers. I raised my hand and the Welcoming gentleman handed me a leaflet, which I left on the seat. We sang a couple of songs that I'd never heard before, and then a sort of séance took place. The couple from behind the altar were calling people from the past, apparently names of loved ones who were already dead.

After the hour-long candle lit service, I realised the place was not the place I was looking for.

I hurried to the door and the Welcoming gentleman caught me. *"Did that help?"* he beamed.

"No, I'm afraid not. The spirit which I encountered was far more friendly. He seemed alive, and not dead," I claimed.

I then thanked him and said good bye.

Little did I know, that not long after, I was to encounter the same Holy Spirit in my awakening.

Fire on the beach

As the weeks went by without any substantial income on the drug trade, I thought it was time again to do some hard labour.

A friend of mine, Glen, was doing well in his building business. So instead of sitting in the pub all day, I asked him if I could have a start. I knew Glen was doing a big rebuild along at Warrior Square, St. Leonards, so he would need some hands on. Glen let me work with the plumbers as a plumber's mate.

Conveniently forgetting my past disasters in the college, I was confident with the little experience I had at plumbing.

Besides, I thought it was an opportunity for me to learn more. I'd never heard of the new plastic push-fit pipework being used in those days. It's called Hep-2-0. It's a great invention. Easy, as you just need to push-fit it into place, no soldering was needed and it was bendy too. I would be working with 'Exocet Mick' and his partner, Ron. Why the nickname, 'Exocet'? Well, Mick had been on board a merchant navy ship which was hit by an Exocet missile in the 1982 Falklands war. Hence he earned the nickname, 'Exocet Mick'.

Mick is a lovely man. A bonus on the job was that we were ripping out all the old copper and lead piping, along with all the existing wiring. I had the job of burning all the plastic off the wiring. This was so we would get a better price for it at the scrap yard.

At the end of the working week, I had arranged for an open back builder's transit truck to pick up all the wires that needed burning off. After loading that Friday afternoon, the truck was full of the stuff. I asked Andrew, the driver, to take me to the Old Town, where there was a waste burning area.

We drove onto the Fisherman's Stade to where we had the booty tipped off. I then went about to ask one of the lads for some diesel or petrol to help the fire start. It was a mighty fine pile, so it was. I doused it all over with half a gallon of petrol, rubbing my hands together with glee. I lit a match and threw it on top of our wee gold mine. Not expecting such a combustible reaction, I was almost blown off my feet but was delighted that, at least, it burned well.

From my inferno, there were huge billows of smoke puffing up into the sky, up and up the billows went. It wasn't long before I heard fire sirens ringing out and coming my way along the seafront. I even wondered where they might be going.

I soon found out. They headed straight towards me. Both came screeching to a halt. The fire team, headed by an attractive young lady, got out from their wagons and approached me. They told me that they'd been called by a worried local and had been informed that the whole fleet of Hastings fishing boats and the entire beach looked like they were on fire.

"*I can understand why, but don't worry, I've got it under control,*" I told the Fire Officers with confidence.

One replied, inspecting the copper wires, "W*ell, looks like it, but you might be getting a fine from the Hastings Borough Council's pollution control unit soon for polluting the air.*"

I managed to quip in jest, "*That would not surprise me at all. I think we'll soon all be paying for the air we breathe.*"

They were amused and took it all as part of a good day's work.

It took a good hour or so before the copper wires were burnt down enough to take to the Old Town scrap merchants.

With the help of one of the boys, we pushed it up the Bourne Road piled up on a market fish cart to the scrap yard, and we got a fair price for it too.

We all had a very good time that weekend with compliments from Glen Reddy Builders.

CHAPTER 20

Downward spiral and continuous brushes with death

I always had a feeling I was living on borrowed time. In reality, we all are.

All around me there was a barrage of disasters, deaths and emotional pain. Something needed to change but instead of a good change, I turned from bad to worse. I was helpless and rendered paralyzed by this monster inside of me. I thought it wanted me dead.

The deaths of my friends brought me to the lowest of my lowest.

Day by day, I was downing a bottle of vodka and sniffing cocaine like it was going out of fashion. A habit that was financed by selling the white pure crystals to the well-off. I would chop it with icing sugar, to make it go further. What I sold was said to be of better quality than most people were selling.

Drugs cause paranoia. I was becoming so paranoid that I had a burglar alarm system fitted in my flat, which I had a mortgage on with the Council.

Late one night, while sitting alone playing my music, it flashed through my mind that the man who lived upstairs owed me money. So, I staggered up the stairs and started banging on his door. My neighbour came to the door.

I lunged at him screaming, *"I want my money!"*

We had a tussle from which he managed to shut me out of his flat, calling me a lunatic.

Going back home, I was furious. The stairwell had large pane glass windows. Drunk, demented and out of my head in an insane rage, I punched my hand straight through one of the windows nearest to me. It wasn't a straight punch, but it was more like a loop over and downwards.

I managed to cut my main artery. As I looked down onto my forearm, the blood pumped, spurting upwards like a fountain. This was made more severe, because my heart beat was beating faster from the exercise of climbing the stairs and having a fight with my neighbour.

I looked with horror. I realised that if I didn't get to a hospital within minutes, I would be dead. I would bleed out.

I had no phone, no car at that time, and the hospital was almost two miles away. The only thing I could do was grasp my forearm to try to stem the blood flow. There was no time to waste, I began to walk three or four hundred yards to The Shah pub in Mount Pleasant Road. I got there reasonably quickly.

The pub was closed so I banged on the door. Fortunately, the owners' dog did not stop barking. So, they came and opened the door to see what all the fuss was about. They kindly let me in and immediately rang up an ambulance. Quick thinking, Robin rushed to get a tie then tightly bound it around my upper forearm. It wasn't long before the ambulance men arrived.

By now I was beginning to feel light headed, I was about to pass out. The ambulance men kept telling me, *"Don't go to sleep, Paul, don't go to sleep!"*

The next day, a nurse woke me up. I had a bandage wrapped around a 4-inch wound on my right forearm that had been stitched up. To this day, I have got the scar to prove it.

The nurse said that she had witnessed a miracle that morning.

I would learn later, from my conversion, that it was God who kept me alive.

But because it took a while, I still experienced several brushes with death as a result of avoidable motor vehicle accidents.

The fish and chips wagon

If nothing else, I was a trier. Sometimes, and maybe against my own better judgement nevertheless, I would have a go at most things.

In Hastings, we have a weekly business advertising and what's on magazine publication that was and still is full of stuff to buy, sell and what to do. I considered myself the entrepreneurial type who took risks.

In that week's publication, I spotted a new venture for sale. It was a fish and chip wagon.

"Lovely," I thought. *"This could be the one that could put me back on the straight and narrow way."*

But to be honest, that was the last thing on my mind. I didn't much care how I made money.

I quite liked living on the edge. The van was over in Rye. I went to look at it with a friend of mine, who was also a keen cook and like me needed a fair chance. I paid a good price of £1800 for our new venture.

My friend and I had all the flyers made up, and we had chosen some good areas out in the country, which were big council estates, located miles away from the nearest food outlets, especially fish and chips.

All we needed to do was deliver the leaflets around the areas telling them what times that we would be there. My friend's granddad would supply us with all the fish that we needed. We were onto a winner.

Leaflets were printed. Next day, we were to go out and start priming the areas for business. But first we decided to celebrate in advance, in my friend Joe's night club. Joe and his family were good to me during my boxing days and he treated me like his own son.

Anyways, my friend parked the van on Joe's newly tarmacked driveway.

Halfway through the night, Joe came in and said, *"Paul, your wagon is sinking in my newly-laid tarmac driveway!"*

So, I told my friend, *"We'd better move the van."*

We'd both had a few drinks and both as high as kites.

As my friend reversed the van out of the drive, and in my enthusiasm, I said, *"Let's have a spin round town and show off the van."*

Not finished there, we decided to drive along the sea front.

Just before we got to Taff's fish and chip shop, coming up on our left, before the traffic lights, my friend took his hand off the steering wheel.

He threw them up in the air, shouting, and mimicking from 'Only Fools and Horses', *"We're going to be millionaires,"* and, at the same time, laughing his head off.

Two seconds later, we ploughed straight into the bus stop. Then even worse, as if it could not get any worse, we crashed our way straight through the fence, down the embankment and into the Combe Haven River.

In my mind, our beloved fish and chip wagon, along with the 'we will be coming to your area soon' leaflets, drifted down the river and out of sight forever.

Not a word was spoken as we both trudged, wet but alive, sloshing our way back home.

That night, I was a very sad man, and no words could describe what I felt. There was only one consolation. The wagon was insured. I eventually got all my money back. Only twenty-five pounds was deducted. Ridiculous as it seems, they deducted £25 because I had taken the battery out after it was towed away to the scrap yard.

I needed it for my car. The cost? Twenty-five pounds.

When would I ever learn?

The dumper

He was a jolly hard-working fellow and built like a mountain. George fixed holes on roads. With the fish and chips wagon gone down the drain, I needed something else to do to get me out from the monotony of my town's clown lifestyle.

I asked him if he could do with a labourer. He said he had a big job going on up near Heathrow airport at an oil refinery. Lots of tarmacking to do. We drove up at the crack of dawn on the Monday, as arranged.

Most of us in the van were worse for wear from the night before. Hardly a word was spoken for the two-and-a-half-hour drive. We eventually arrived at our destination. It was as George had said, "a big job."

I was given some protective clothing with a hard hat and boots. There were machines, metal structures, offices in Portacabins and men at work, moving around like industrious ants. The work place, wherever it was, was teaming with activity.

My job was to get the newly-mixed tarmac from where it had been prepared to where it was to be laid. Initially, I was using a wheel barrow, but then I spotted an unmanned dumper truck which I thought would do the job quicker and easier. I'd never driven a dumper truck before, but hey, this had an ignition key in it, a gearbox, with clutch and brakes just like my car. So, driving it, I thought, would be a piece of cake.

This machine was twice the size of the normal dumpers I had seen. So, I thought it would be best if I take it for a spin round the yard first to get the hang of it. Climbing up onto the single seat was a bit of a struggle. But once I'd got up there, I put my hands on the large steering wheel, took a few deep breaths, checked if it was out of gear then started her up. It looked straight forward to manoeuvre. There was a lever with an arrow that pointed up and down for the front bucket. It worked well. Hydraulic it was. *"Ummm, let's have a test drive."*

So, foot on clutch into first gear, lightly easing my foot up on the clutch, hand brake off, and away we went.

I put my foot down and shot off for a round trip. I thought it was going to be a really smooth test drive but something happened. I had made a fatal, minor, very stupid mistake.

I didn't notice the 'the slow down hump' which was lying in my path. As I hit the hump, this very large dumper truck went out of control, sending me off course bouncing to my left. We bounced at some speed crashing straight into an on-site pay telephone kiosk. *"Thank, goodness, no one was in it."*

Then the dumper continued to smash its way into the administration's Portacabin site office. It caused quite a stir.

Fortunately, nobody was hurt.

That was the end of my tarmacking career. George was not too pleased, either.

That weekend, in the pub. George and I got into an argument about my disastrous performance. I called him a pig and stormed out of the pub. He came after me and grabbed me by the throat. He picked me up and shook me like a rag doll, then dropped me to the ground. He then made his way over to the betting shop.

I came to my senses, feeling I needed to retain some sort of defence for my reputation. I felt belittled, so I went over to confront big George. I looked up at him with tears in my eyes, and said', *"What did you do that for?"* I then reached out my right hand up onto his left shoulder as a measuring stick, and then 'as fast as lightning', unleashed a thundering left hook that was placed square on George's jaw. I was only a little over ten stone and 5'6". George, on the other hand, was 20 stone, he was a very big lad.

Down went dear George. I liked him and I was worried that he might die, as he laid out cold in the busy seafront pavement.

After a minute or two, there was still no movement from George.

In desperation, I got down on my knees and began to give George the kiss of life. He wasn't the sort of man that would kiss another man, but he soon became conscious.

"I'm sorry, George. I am very glad that you're still with us."

I continued, *"Come and see me some time, I'll buy you a pint."*

Off I went before he was on his feet, thinking, *"I don't fancy those big hands round my throat again."*

Another car accident

Another friend of mine, Jack, told me that there was a rave going on in London and he had two free tickets for us. It was being organised by KISS-FM, a London radio station, and an extra bonus for me was that two boxing colleagues of mine were going to be there too, British Champion Gary Mason. I liked Gary. He was a great fighter, winning thirty-seven of his thirty-eight fights; and Nigel Ben, the middle-weight world champion, would be there as well. Nigel was the DJ that night.

Friday came, I picked up my friend, and off we went. It doesn't take long to get to the centre of London from Hastings. On a good run, it would probably take two hours. We left Hastings early so we could be prepared for any delays on the road.

Driving through London can be a nightmare if you're not used to it. I knew my way into Central London, but from there I had no idea how to get to the venue. Back then, Sat-Navs were unheard of, so we decided to park where we could.

London is a great place to visit, and is better on foot. After a bit of sight-seeing, we found our way to the venue. What struck me straight away was a real live-size fairground carousel in the middle of the place, which everyone was going round and round on, while the heavy drum 'n' bass were thumping on. Gary was at the bar.

As time went by, I remained relatively sober. Near midnight, Jack and I had decided we had had enough. We both had plans for the next day. So, thanking our new friends, we returned to the car for our journey back home.

Being dark, it wasn't clear which way we had to go, but after asking a friendly policeman we soon found our way out onto the south circular. Then to Bromley and out onto the A21. From there, it was a straight drive home.

There was no rush. Jack, by now had fallen asleep, so I put on some classical music which is good listening on a run.

Everything was going fine until we reached Robertsbridge.

The approach into Robertsbridge is a long, winding hill that takes you to the roundabout. I was tired, my eyes were heavy, on our way down and going at some speed, I dozed off. My head just dropped.

This was the amazing part. A voice, from where I don't know, but it was audible or was it in my head, but it was a voice. Maybe an angel, but I heard, *"Wake up Paul, you're just about to crash."* I lifted my head up immediately and saw that I was going off onto the gravel towards the trees, and quickly I turned the wheel hard right, but it was too late. The voice or 'my angel' then said, *"Hold yourself into your seat Paul, now!"*

So instantaneously, I grabbed the bottom of the steering wheel and pushed myself hard into my seat. In the meantime, our car began to roll. The windscreen came crashing in. I could hear and feel the car rolling, over and over. The roof was being ripped into pieces. We went from the left of the road rolling over to the right.

Then again, I heard the voice, *"Let go of the wheel now Paul."*

I did as I was told. I felt as if a hand had grabbed me by my shirt collar, and then lifted me from the car as it was still moving and then sat me down softly on the side of the road's grass verge.

The car was smashed to pieces, but back on it's wheels.

Jack was saved by the seat belt, groaning but alive. A lorry pulled up and came to our rescue. The man called an ambulance on his mobile. I thanked the man and said, *"Please stay with Jack until the ambulance comes."*

With his assurance that he would and still in shock, I walked across the road and disappeared up into the fields towards a farmhouse that had its lights on. By the time I had got to the farmhouse, its lights were off and so I got into an open car in the driveway. I looked back across the way I had come and could see flashing blue lights. An ambulance was on its way from the Robertsbridge ambulance station.

I heard a helicopter searching overhead. It was hovering around, obviously looking for me. I decided to just lie there and pass the night. I was not in the mood to talk to any police officers and was still in shock.

Morning came and from my hilltop position, I could see the village called Robertsbridge which was maybe half a mile away. I couldn't see the car through the trees down at the bottom of the fields. I didn't really want to. I felt terribly ashamed but also wondered, *"Who was really saving me all my life from dying?"*

With the numerous near-death encounters, both through my own folly, and some accidental, I should have died a long time ago. But someone just steps in to save me.

When I got home there was an official police note that had been put through my letterbox. It read, *"Please get in touch with Bexhill Police Station as soon as you get this notice."*

I rang the police, and they asked me to come and see them at their Bexhill Station and something about collecting my road tax disc, as I could be refunded the money back as it was new. I inquired about Jack and they said he was in a better shape after being treated at the hospital, saved only by his seatbelt.

I promised to come the next day.

Upon arriving that very next day, I was taken by police car to a yard where they showed me my vehicle. The Officer was surprised to see me without as much as a scratch apart from a slight abrasion that I had on my forehead, where the shattered windscreen glass had caught me.

The Officer asked, *"How on earth did you manage to get out of this alive?"*

I was drawn to tell him the story. He listened with interest, but alas, not only was I going to be marked down as a wanted man later, but a nutcase too. I didn't care but being accused of murdering someone would soon totally change my life.

I had to pay a cost for the tow truck. Another right-off insurance claim was on the cards.

Oh well, Jack was alive and so was I.

All thanks to my Angel?

CHAPTER 21

The accusation

Five or six years before the millennium of 2000, I thought it would be a great idea to form a travel agency called 'Millennium Tours.' We had a lot of fun with that for a while. I used to arrange tickets and coach trips to the London's West end theatre and musical performances, and we'd also go to dog racing events. We also offered rave parties.

At the same time, my drug dealing continued and by now I had financed a weed growing basement flat in St. Leonards. It was a nice, quiet operation that only two of us knew about. It brought in a nice amount of cash each month and an on-tap supply of strong skunk weed.

Most of the time, I was stoned out of my deteriorating skull. I would be drinking and smoking weed from my pipe every day from when I woke up, until the early hours of the next morning.

One day, I was standing at the bar, which we used as our base for meetings and having a nice pint, when to my surprise, two plain-clothed police officers came and stood one either side of me at the bar.

They were dressed in everyday clothes that blended in well with what was the norm. One of the officers showed me his ID and said, *"We need to have a talk with you Paul, up at the station."*

I replied, in a matter of fact and relaxed as possible way, *"OK, not a problem. Would you like a pint before we go?"* They did.

We then went and sat down at an empty window table. *"What's the problem?"* I asked.

"Just routine," they replied. "But we want to talk to you about the murder of Bobby Jones." This came as a shock. I hardly knew Bobby Jones.

The question also brought me back to my senses. I realised that I had an ounce of skunk weed in my pocket. So, I thought it would be a good idea to first dismiss myself to the toilet. I went to the men's cubical and, in a bit of a panic, I took a package from my inside jacket pocket and put it into the flushing overhead cistern.

I returned to the Police Officers and we finished our beers and left for the police station, which was only 700 yards or so away.

In the car, there was a distinctive and very strong aroma of skunk weed that was filling up the vehicle.

The Officer turned to me and asked, *"Do you smoke weed, Paul?"*

I replied, *"Well I must admit officer, that I have tried it once or twice when I was in Amsterdam, who doesn't?"*

"Ummm," came the reply.

I struggled with the smell. I thought, *"Where was this coming from?"* while checking my inside pocket. To my horror, I realised that, in my panic back at the pub, I had put the wrong package into the cistern. The package I had hidden had been a bag of jelly babies. I was fond of jelly babies and had them everywhere.

I was led into the station through a security door then up a flight of stairs. I asked the Officer if I could go to the toilet again. This time, the larger of the two men followed me in. I went into the open cubical and stuffed the money bag full of weed package down the front of my track suit bottoms. I thought that was the safest place to hide it.

As the officer was following me along to the interview room, the package slowly slipped down the leg of my baggy track suit bottoms then out in full view of the officer. *"I've had it,"* I thought.

But the Officer calmly told me to pick the incriminating item up and put it in my pocket, with his final words,

"This is a murder inquiry."

I was taken into an interview room where the officers asked me a few questions about Bobby Jones and where I was on the night of the murder. I did my best to recall my drunken stoned three or four weeks that had passed since the killing took place in Alexandra Park.

I explained, again, that I did not personally know the deceased man, but I did know of him as a street dealer and that he worked with the gypsies. *"I'm sorry, I can't tell you what I don't know."*

The interview was relatively brief. I was then allowed to go.

The Officers kindly arranged a police car to take me back to the pub. I was excited to tell the story to the boys. I went and got my jelly babies.

For me, back then, it was a great relief that they let me go with the weed. Not that I have not been charged in the past, because as I have mentioned my DBS is 7 to 8 pages long. The murder squad obviously had more important things to do.

That same week, a man called Anthony had come round my house and asked if I wanted to purchase a double barrel shot gun.

I liked the idea of owning a gun and so I bought it. I sawed it down into a handy tool that could be easily concealed. I hid it under my fridge with a small bag of cartridges.

CHAPTER 22

The vicious attack and the shotgun

The weekend after I bought the shot gun, I had a couple of halves of Directors bitter on a nice mid-summer sunny Saturday afternoon in 1995 in my favourite pub.

On the balcony, was a lady doing sponsored haircuts for a local charity. I needed a haircut, so I asked if I could go next. While I was having my hair cut, a very tall man with short dark hair came walking up the concrete stairs of the pub that I was in. As he passed by, for no reason, made fun and called me a *'girly poof.'*

Then looking down at me, and in a Liverpool accent, said, *"Are you a poof, mate?"*

I never said a word back. I didn't even know the man and so I asked the lady to finish my hair cut, which she did. I thanked her for her good service, and walked back into the pub.

To my surprise, the man was still there and continued taunting. I wasn't too pleased with this stranger's persistent taunts. So, I walked up to him, gently reached out my right hand putting it onto his left shoulder. Then with my left hand clenched into a tight fist and, like lightning, I crashed it as in a hook shot directly onto his jaw.

He went down, but was still conscious. The man could take a good shot. There were a few heated words exchanged and then he left.

I didn't see the man again until later that evening. He had shrewdly waited watching with his spies until I was hardly able to stand up. Without notice, the back bar doors flew open.

Then I was attacked by two or three men. I was pinned to the bar floor. The big man bit my face and had a firm bite hold on my nose. The other man trapped one of my legs in the door.

I was helpless and could not move.

The man eventually managed to bite part of my nose off. At the same time, the other men tried to get me into the waiting van, which was outside. I was able to hold my ground, with some super strength surging through my body.

If they had managed to get me into the back of the van, I was told they were going to club hammer me to death.

They had to get away fast before the police arrived, whom the bar man, I later learned, had called.

A kind Officer told me that the 'columella' part of my nose had been bitten off (that's the part that separates the nostrils), and he'd asked the bar man for some ice and wrapped the end piece of my nose with the ice into a clean handkerchief. I was taken to the hospital and there I had a skin graft. The skin was surgically taken from the back of my ear to try and straighten my nose out.

My nose is a bit crooked since then. It would be something I would have to live with, for the rest of my life. Of course, once I thought about it, the incident could have been related to my drug related activities. I just was not sure, how exactly it was so, then.

I was glad to have purchased a gun. I realised I would have the opportunity to use it. I was enraged and wanted revenge.

Atter a month went by, and the stiches were taken out of my nose, I investigated who the man and the gang were.

I discovered that the man was connected to the Merseyside Liverpudlian gangs and that if and when he was in town, he possibly might drink in the Pig in Paradise pub on the Hastings sea front.

One dark evening just before closing time, I loaded up both barrels of my shot gun and sat across from the pub, waiting for the man, ready to kill.

I was continuously being encouraged by Mr. Destroyer to avenge myself.

I was evil, and, hell bent for revenge with a balaclava over my head, I waited.

He never came.

While sitting in the shadows, I came to my senses. *"This was madness,"* I realised.

I went back home and put the gun away. To be honest, I might have been a Devil's child back then but I don't think I had it in me to kill. But that treasured shotgun would soon lead me to prison.

CHAPTER 23

The arrest

This is how I got to prison.

I had a good friend, who lived in Hollington with his girlfriend. I would spend many evenings in their house. We got on well.

It was probably 6 or 7 am in the morning. From my friend's settee, I picked up the Hastings Observer and began reading about the Bobby Jones recent murder in the park. The story for the second week running was now on the front page.

Suddenly, crashing through my friend's back door came armed police Officers shouting, *"Don't move"*.

I noticed all sorts of men and women, some in uniform and some not. The two men who had taken me up to the station only a few weeks back were leading this arrest. With all entrances guarded, I was told that I was under arrest on suspicion of murdering Bobby Jones. I was then read my rights.

My friend was now down from his bedroom. The Officers were about to handcuff me, but I insisted that was not necessary.

"Trust me, I said. It's OK. "

As I was being led out of the front door, I called my friend and gave him permission to talk to the police and tell them everything he knew. My friend knew I was not the killer.

I was taken to Bexhill Police Station, then searched. My house front door keys were taken, shoes removed and then I was locked in a cell.

I asked to see my Solicitor or a Solicitor, whoever was available. I had been convicted of so many crimes in the past but have never murdered anyone. Surely, this was a very serious accusation.

A duty Solicitor eventually did turn up, but stood outside of the cell door. From there, he opened the hatch and began to ask me silly questions and saying things like, *"Don't worry, Paul, we will get you off this murder. Just tell me, what time of the night did you do it and we can fix things around that."*

Immediately, I became suspicious of this lawyer's intentions and ability. Why would he assume that I did it?

I went up to the door and squeezed my head out as far as my eyes could see along the corridor. I noticed that the police officers were listening to our conversation.

"Get me another solicitor!" I demanded, adding, angrily, *"Disgusting behaviour!"*

As the day went by, the father of lies, Mr. Destroyer, was whispering, *"These police Officers have wanted you for such a long time. They are willing to make anything up just to have you locked away, forever."* Understandably, because I was a clear menace to society.

Later that day, two officers came into my cell and produced my sawn-off shot gun with the cartridges. They had been to, and searched, my home.

They then began to explain why I had been arrested.

I was told that while investigating and combing the park area for evidence, the searching Officers had found a torn bail sheet with my previous conviction and with my name on it. This sheet was in the vicinity of the crime. Immediately, it came to mind how that bail sheet had got there.

A few days beforehand, I had explained in detail, *"After a night in my friend's, I was going to my girlfriend's house, who is the mother of my son Louis. Kelly's place was by the park. On the way, I was caught short, so needed to have a dump. It was early, and no one was around, so I went into the bush, had a dump and wiped my backside on the portion of the bail sheet paper. It was the only* paper I found in the deep end of one of the pockets of my trousers."

I went on, *"As I came out from the bush, I remember I saw someone I knew, who was walking his Staffordshire cross bull terriers close by."*

I had a chat with him and then went off to Kelly's.

With that explanation, they asked, *"Do you remember where you had your dump?"*

"Yes, I think so," I replied.

"So, you won't mind if we go and you show us then, Paul," The arresting officer said. *"Not a problem,"* I replied. I was then handcuffed. *"Is this necessary?"* I asked again.

"Yes, it is," they insisted.

"Now, let's go," said the Officer.

We drove the five miles to the park, in silence. I advised them to stop in St. Helen's Road, which runs down beside the park. We got out of the battered old marina car. I led the way in handcuffs to the park bushes. I knew the park well.

After a brief search around, I found the bush where I'd had the dump in. *"There it is!"* I exclaimed.

"That's it then," said the Officer.

"What do you mean, that's it then?" I asked. *"Dig it up, if you don't believe me!"* I insisted.

"That won't be necessary," replied the Officer." *The rain would have washed it all away."*

Very much confused, I just blabbered on, *"Then check the bail sheet for DNA and go and talk with Tony with the dogs. He knew I was here, but not to kill a man."*

We drove back to Bexhill, from where I was charged with possession of a sawn-off firearm without a license, instead of the murder charge they were trying to pin down on me.

I was released on bail pending further investigations and told not to leave the country.

I was scheduled to appear at Lewis Crown Court the following month for the sentencing.

CHAPTER 24

The sentencing

Court day had arrived. It was getting past the summer months of 1995.

Early that morning, I locked up my flat, turned on the burglar alarm system and thought that I wouldn't be seeing the light of day on Civvy Street for a long while.

I said my last goodbyes to family and friends. It was the end. I had fallen from a great height. They finally got me for the long haul.

Before I left, I put my best handmade silk suit on with a Ben Sherman Shirt and tie. My old-fashioned 1930s gold hunter pocket watch and chain were tucked into my waistcoat pocket. I finished off my attire with my 'highly polished' brown leather pair of brogues, which I wore for special occasions. Oh, and a pair of Ray-Ban shades.

I told myself that If I was going to be locked up for a long time, I'd just as well have to do it in style.

I decided to take the time to reflect while on my train journey to Lewes. I do have moments, especially on occasions such as these, when I pondered on the future, and even the big, empty void, inside of me, which I have always felt the need to fill. Whatever it was, whoever it might be, I needed to find out who can fill it. I needed to find out very soon or I would die.

Arriving at the court house had been a long climb from Lewes train station. I knew my way well. It was all uphill. I was met by my Solicitor, Joe. I'd had Joe on many other court appearances.

He was a wise, knowledgeable man and one of the best defence lawyers in town.

Joe told me that I had a judge who didn't like guns. His name was Justice Brown. With that, I should expect a four to seven-year sentence.

After being formally registered on my arrival and told what court room I would be sentenced in, I was then taken to the courtroom's holding cells. These cells are down in the dungeons. I was put in a large holding area with other prisoners who were waiting to be called for sentencing.

I went and found a quiet corner, where I could pray. I began to plead to Jesus or God or whoever it might be that everybody else prays to in churches. I was desperate. I did not want to be locked up for 7 years in jail.

I was pleading to whoever might be listening in the heavens above, *"Please Jesus, God or whoever you are. if you're a real God, you know I'm not that bad. Yes, I'm bad, but like Mum says, I'm a Dr. Jekyll and Mr. Hyde. I want to do well and yet, I love doing bad too, but, but, but please Lord help me Lord. I promise I will do my best in future."*

My prayer sincerely went on, *"If only you might help me out here, just a bit. Please, Jesus."*

I looked around the holding cell. Judge Brown's name was etched everywhere. "Judge Send 'em' down Brown gave me fifteen years"; "Send 'em' down Brown gave me twenty-five years" and on it went.

"God, please help me!" I continued to plead.

It was time to face the music. The jailer opened our cell door. I was called for judgement.

The jailer led me up and into the courtroom.

I was told to sit on the accused's bench. There was a shout. *"Court arise!'"*

We all stood up while Judge send 'em' down Brown came in and made himself comfortable. He then gestured with his hand that we may sit.

I looked around the courtroom. There were a lot of police officers, both plain-clothed and in uniform placed behind me. They looked like a group of praying mantises dressed in uniform. I felt that I was about to be devoured.

I looked forward, bowed my head, and prayed some more under my breath as the proceedings began,

"This was doom's day, for most of us here in this court room," I thought. On and on it went.

Finally, Judge Brown told me to stand up, while leafing through the reams of my past court appearances.

He peered over the top of his glasses at me. *"Mr. Huggins you have led a past life of failures. You have been a victim of your own demise, but something is telling me that there is light for you at the end of the tunnel. But,"* he added, *"you need to buckle down and get away from this criminal lifestyle. So for your stupidity, therefore, today I'm going to give you nine..."*

There was a long pause, a very long pause. Finally, Mr. Justice Brown said, ***"9 Months prison in her Majesty's custody!*** *I don't want to be seeing you here again. Take him down."*

I was thrilled to bits. I put both arms in the air with the Winston Churchill style V signs. I looked into Mr. Justice Browns eyes, and said, almost shouting, *"Thank you and God bless you, your Honour!"*

I turned to the police, as if they were really my enemies and smiled. They all looked stunned.

I went down with the jailer to await my transport that would take me around the corner to HMP Lewes.

Something amazing had just happened to me. I was given even lower than the minimal sentence.

A sudden realization also dawned on me: Jesus saves and truly answers prayers.

As you are about to find out, this was going to be the beginning of my wonderful relationship with our Saviour, Jesus Christ.

Prison would be the first step to real freedom.

PART 3:

____

TRANSFORMATION, THE UPS AND DOWNS IN MY CHRISTIAN LIFE, FINDING THE LOVE OF MY LIFE, AND THE LESSONS OF MY LIFE.

CHAPTER 25

Awakening by the Holy Spirit

Later that day, those of us from the holding cells who received custodial sentences were led up and into the awaiting sweat wagon. We were driven a short distance to HMP Lewes, East Sussex.

Like most other penitentiaries, the castle-like entrance was somewhat demeaning. You are brought to book, given a number, and then dressed the same as everyone else. You eat the same food and follow the same rules, orders and routines. I was rendered a nobody.

The cells were approximately 12ft long by 8ft wide and whitewashed throughout with graffiti on the walls of some prisoners' past. Etchings of calendars counting the days to when they might see the light of day and their loved ones again were common. There was also a small box room that has a toilet. Both cell and toilet areas had spy holes. The dark blue heavy metal cell door had a latch where items can be passed through to you. You have a small square window at the back of the cell, which was heavily barred, with flies flying in and out. I was watching the flies and figured that if I were one of them, I could escape.

This was the environment that I needed to adjust to. Yes, I had received a miraculous 9-month sentence which gave me comfort of sorts. So, on reflection, I was determined to wake up and use this time of incarceration as a medicine rather than a punishment.

At first, I was locked in my cell for almost 23 hours each day. I had a cell mate who didn't talk much, which suited me just fine.

He kept himself to himself, and he was quiet and polite. For some there could be nothing worse than being in such a confined space with a confrontational bully. I quickly learned that I could get a day job. Any job would do, just get me out of this cell. I took the first job opportunity that came along. Jobs of your choice were sparse for obvious reasons. I took a job in one of the workshops that made brooms. My job was to stick the broom heads onto the handles. We were given a small wage at the end of each week that we could use for buying some tobacco, a phone card and other bits and bobs like sugar, powdered milk and tea bags.

On Sundays, there was an opportunity to go to chapel. For most of us. this was just another chance to get out of the cells and for others it's a place where you could exchange things like drugs, which were smuggled in. Drugs and tobacco were the main currencies in jail.

I was determined to stay away from such dealings. I wanted to get out of there as quickly as possible and needed to be on my best behaviour. Drug tests were frequent procedures and if you tested positive, extra time was the penalty for your actions.

I didn't know at the time, but a well-known boxer from Brighton was one of the church ministers at Lewes. Terry Tulley was his name. Unfortunately, I was moved to another jail before I got to meet him.

I was in Lewes jail for no more than 3 or 4 weeks. I was then told, 'without notice', that I was to be shipped out to Camp Hill prison that day. Camp Hill is situated on the Isle of Wight. I heard that my new destination was an easy-going prison with the opportunity to learn a trade of some sort. I was told to go pack my kit in my pillow case and report to the landing officer. I was then taken to a holding cell and given my civvy clothes to put on. Then an hour later, I was herded into a sweat wagon that was going to take us down to Gosport ferry crossing. The trip from Lewes to

Gosport is a 2-hour road journey, depending on the flow of traffic.

As I've previously mentioned, I suffer from claustrophobia. I hated being locked in that tiny cubical. I was suffocating for 2 whole hours and dreading the thought of an accident, then only to be burnt to death.

At last, we arrived at Gosport. We were handcuffed then herded onto the ferry. Gosport to Camp Hill prison, which was a further 27 miles away.

Upon arrival, my civvy clothes were taken away. I went through the usual hygiene wash in the bath house, where I was then given prison clothes and a hygiene pack. I was then shown to a holding room until designated to a house dormitory.

In the holding room, the prison Chaplain came and gave me a Good News Bible, which had pictures and diagrams in it. It was brand new and had a nice shiny hard back cover. I thanked the nice Chaplain and promised that I would read it.

In fact, not only would I read this Good News Bible. I wanted to study it and find out who this God or Jesus was. I wanted an explanation or a revelation of who it was who had kept me alive through numerous near-death experiences over the past years.

Camp Hill prison, and its reforms, were much like that of a borstal. Relatively easy and offering plenty of opportunities to better yourself, both intellectually, and through a trade, because of further education classes. Trades ranged from bricklaying to car mechanics.

Unfortunately, my stay at Camp Hill was not long enough to establish a realistic plan. I was once again told, and without notice, that I would be moved to HM prison Wandsworth, south west of London.

After going through the same old prison routine and having to endure the claustrophobic torture of travelling for hours in the sweat box. We at last arrived at our destination. HMP Wandsworth was built in 1851. It was old and dingy. The cells were even smaller than they were in HMP Lewes. Humiliating as it was. All of us prisoners, all one thousand eight hundred and seventy-seven of us, had to slop out our waste products from our chamber pots. Our landing doors would be opened each morning and off we would go to empty our smelly slush in the slop rooms. No luxuries of having a toilet in our cells in Wandsworth.

After I had been put into a cramped cell, I was told yet again, a couple of weeks later, to pack my kit to be moved to HMP Wormwood Scrubs, in West London! I was beginning to think that I was a prisoner on Her Majesty's tour.

After going through the repetitive prison systems formalities, I was placed in a cell on the third landing with a man called, David, who was serving an 18 months sentence. It was early in the year of 1996. I liked David. We would play endless games of chess. He was a business man in the Antique industry. It was David's first ever prison sentence. He got a sentence for possession of an ounce of cocaine. David could finish off a Daily Telegraph crossword in under 15 minutes. He had been his school's chess champion. I beat him, but once only in the many games we played. He was a nice man, with not a hurtful bone in his body.

Without notice, I was then moved in with another prisoner across the landing. His name was Bill. Bill told me that he was a heroin dealer who had pulled a gun out on his arresting police officer. He was apprehended without firing a shot and given 8 years for his trouble. It was in Bill's cell that something very special was about to happen.

One afternoon we were doing the usual chill out that came after our one hour 'on the yard' exercise. Back in our cell and locked up, Bill was listening to his radio, that just so happened to be playing a song by Joan Osborne called, *'What if God Was One of Us'*. I was reading my Good News Bible. Part of the song's lyrics go like this;

If God had a face, what would it look like?
And would you want to see
if seeing meant that you would have to believe
in things like heaven and in Jesus and the saints
and all the prophets?

In my Bible, I was at the beginning of the book of John. If you were once, like me, an unbeliever, John is in the New Testament Gospels. The opening words of that first chapter are these: *"In the beginning was the Word, and the Word was with God, and the Word was God. He was in the beginning with God. All things were made through Him, and without Him nothing was made that was made. In Him was life, and the life was the light of men. And the light shines in the darkness, and the darkness did not comprehend it."* (John 1:1-5).

It was then that I reflected back to my near-death experiences and pondered on the undeniable and personal supernatural encounters which I had. I thought, *"It must have been Jesus who was behind those very real encounters."* I wanted to know who Jesus is. So, I just began to pray, whatever was in my mind and heart, *"Dear Jesus. In this Bible, these written words are telling me that you are God. Are you truly God? Please, can you show me more evidence? I like this book, but it's a book. I want to know you more Lord. I'm so sorry that I've been so bad over the years. I want to change, but I do not know how to. You have saved me in the past, that I truly believe. Can you show me how to change, please?"*

Just then, I became aware of a spiritual force that had, at that moment, entered in through my thinking, my awareness, or whatever it was, then this feeling went down into my heart and then He, 'Jesus', opened my eyes. I became filled with an overwhelming awakening of a knowledge that I cannot describe or begin to put it all down in this book.

Somehow, I was given a bird's eye view, a 'vision' if you like, of God's creation and Our Creator, and why we were created. It dawned on me there and then, in that prison cell's upper bunk bed, that Jesus Christ loves me and wants a real-life relationship with me. Through the reading of the Bible, God made me understand the greatest gift, which had been given to the sinful mankind: His Son, Jesus Christ. Jesus came down to live and become one of us, so He could fulfill God the Father's plan to save us from our sins.

Right there and then, I had no doubt that Jesus Christ was the one saving me in the past. He was and is my, and our, Saviour.

I began to cry. I could not control the tears, rolling down my face. *"I'm born again,"* I shouted out. *"I'm born again!* I didn't even know what born again was or meant, I just felt new. I really felt I had become new. 'Born again'!

Bill, surprised at my sudden outburst, looked up and asked, *"What the 'bleep' are you talking about Paul?"*

"This Bible," I replied. *"This Bible. It's all true."* Bill was none too amused, *"Whatever."* said Bill, then returned to his music.

I, and in God's perfect timing, on the other hand, had just experienced a miraculous re-birth. Jesus had personally touched me in that moment and showed me who He is, was, and is to come. I felt new. I felt changed.

I thought, *"I am going to have a new start in life. Jesus would help me."*

Through the years as a Christian, I was about to discover that Christianity is a personal relationship with Jesus, who is God. And that it isn't a walk in the park. It is a tough and challenging lifestyle, but God is patient. Even in our worst failings, He is patient and is very much willing to change us. Sanctification over the coming years ahead would prove to be a wonderful and painful experience, as He slowly takes away my filthy habits.

That very next Sunday, I went to the prison chapel worship service. I couldn't wait to tell the Chaplain what had happened to me. Life goes on in prison. I didn't have long to go. Sometimes, if I had any spare tobacco, I would roll a roll up. Then I would get a square piece of writing paper and write a little message on it. Something like, "*Jesus loves you. Have a great day. The best is yet to come.*" Then I added a smiley face. I'd fold the roll up in the paper and then throw it out of my third landing window down onto the exercise yard below. Whichever landing from below was out there having their exercise that morning or afternoon, I would watch one of the inmates pick up the folded paper. It always put a smile on their faces when they found a roll up inside and read the note. It was my small way of witnessing. They never knew it was me.

Once again towards the end of my sentence, I was moved back to HMP Lewes. This was to be my home run.

I had less than a month to go. The day finally arrived in mid-1996. The last weeks' countdown was slow, but time waits for no man. I was about to be free.

My release day finally came. That very morning, I had my bedding and kit all packed, ready. As I waited for my cell door to open, I was holding my breath. I was listening to every footstep that went past my cell door, hoping to hear the jangling of the keys. My tightened stomach muscles relaxed and a sense of utopia filled me with joy as those keys were finally put into the jailer's lock.

I was led to reception, given my clothes and a generous amount of money to see me through the next week or two. I signed my release papers and was taken to the main gate. I turned to one of the screws and shook his hand.

Then, I was gone and free on a beautiful, mid-summer's day.

The view over the West Hill.

CHAPTER 26

Free at last and wrestling with temptations

The train ride to Hastings was delightful. Getting off the train at Hastings station, I went for a stroll. Everything which I had taken for granted like window shopping and buying a simple ice cream were new pleasures. I had missed the simple things.

I walked to my flat. Up and over the West Hill. The views are stunning. I was back home in the town I love.

On the way back to my flat I stopped off and got some nice-smelling cleaning materials. I spent the latter part of that day going through my flat washing the place clean. I felt clean and new. I wanted my flat to be that way too.

A day or so passed, and I went around to see family and friends. Later, there was a knock on my door. An old friend had come round to see me. He presented me with a deal. A big deal, which involved smuggling large amounts of cocaine. It was almost too good to refuse. But there and then, I told him about Jesus. I told him of my conversion experience. That Jesus was now who I was going to follow and so I would not be getting back to my old ways. It is filth and I want nothing to do with it. He left, unconvinced, but I felt good. Someone later shot him but, thankfully, he survived.

I was so thankful that I was now on a new path. Yes, Mr. Destroyer would never go away. He hides in the shadows until an opportune time, but now I was beginning to understand who the Devil really is. He is an angry, cunning, perverted liar, a sadist who hates God and those who belong to Him especially. He disguises himself in many ways, but, as the Bible says, he only comes to steal, kill and destroy. And sadly, he is the Prince of this world. Just look around you. It is plain to see.

I also went and saw Kelly. Sadly, we had split up, but she did not have a problem with me seeing Louis whenever I wanted. I took him over to the swings in the park.

Kelly and Louis eventually moved away to Canterbury,

Now I get to see my wee lad, now in his twenties, more often. But at least now, we have a dad-son relationship of sorts, and I am glad that he is a kind-hearted lad. There's still room for improvement for us both. There is still time.

Recently, I took Louis to church in Canterbury and he seemed to love it. We would continue to pray that the seed planted would grow.

All I can do is pray for the day when all my children would come to know the Lord.

Church

A week or so had passed since my release. I was at a bit of a loose end. I still had my old classic Austin A35 motor. It was a Sunday morning. Fresh on my mind was my conversion to Christianity, but something was missing. I realised what it was. A church to go to.

I prayed for direction and the Lord led me to King's Church, on the Ridge

On my way to church, Mr. Destroyer was furious. He began to whisper, "*You don't want to go to King's Paul, just think of what your friends will say. They would be laughing at you and poking fun.*" The destroyer continued to whisper, "*Look, I've got a better idea. Let's go down to the Nelly and have a drink with the lads. Let's go and just have some fun.*"

At first, I thought, yeah, why not, I can always pop back next week, no worries. I turned Bessey around and began to head back in the opposite direction towards the Old Town. God was having none of it. In my mind, a battle was going on, *"Paul your friends can wait. Besides, up at King's, you will meet lots of new friends, even some which you haven't seen for a long time while at school. Go on, go and see them. Don't forget that you helped build that building when it was used as an indoor cricket pitch. All those foundations you laid in concrete. Go and have a look at the good job you made of it all."*

In the end, I listened to my helper, The Holy Spirit, and drove straight into King's church car park.

King's Church is a big building on the Ridge Road in Hastings. It was built just a couple of years before I'd left prison. The building was originally built as a new 'in vogue' at the time, indoor cricket and badminton facility, which didn't catch on. I was working with the ground workers. We laid the foundations along with the cesspool tanks and drainage for the building. It is now a fine building, which had been modernised throughout, used as a conference centre and the home of King's Church.

As I came in, I was greeted by the friendly doorman and handed a leaflet. By the time 10.30 am came round, the attendance reached way over 300 to 400.

Pastor Dave Lyons was preaching that morning. There was some music, played live by the very capable worship team. It was all very different from what you might expect in a church. The service was very lively, with 'happy, clappy' people enjoying Jesus' songs that weren't from your typical school hymn book.

After the worship, one or two people got up on the stage and shared what was happening in their lives that week.

I felt that God was encouraging me, *"There you go Paul, go and tell them what's happened with us over the past few weeks."*

I didn't hesitate.

From the back I walked to the front and up onto the stage. I was handed the microphone. I happily chatted away for 10 minutes. And finished off with how grateful I was to God, our Lord Jesus, who had brought me into King's Church that morning. I learned that what I did on the stage was called a 'testimony.'

After the one and a half hour or so service, there were tea and biscuits for those who wanted to stay and chat, which was most of us. I met lots of people I knew from both school, work and play. It was great to have begun my humble Christian fellowship beginnings with King's Church. I loved them so much. I stayed for a further 7 years.

It wasn't long before I was having Bible studies and going through the fundamentals with the elders of what Christianity is and what it means in our daily lives.

I was shown the scripture about Baptism. I had a natural desire to be baptized. I wanted to show the world in a statement of faith by way of baptism that I was a new creation. The old was gone, the new had come. I had changed deep down within and I liked the change. I wanted to confess my faith by way of full immersion in the baptismal pool as soon as possible.

I was baptized in November, 1996.

It was great. Being proclaimed a Christian and truly knowing Jesus Christ is my greatest blessing. A treasure, that would last for eternity in heaven.

CHAPTER 27

The miraculous provision through The Entertainer magazine

Back home alone in the week, I realised I wanted a proper job. Yes, it was fantastic that I would never deal in drugs again, but I needed a regular income. I'd washed my hands of everything that I'd been doing before my jail sentence. It was all over and done with. I was doing a bit of plumbing work here and a little labour work there. It was all good and well, but I wanted something that would be more substantial. So, when in need, we need to shout it out to the Lord.

What happened later was a miraculous provision from the Lord.

I was having a beer in the Old Town, just a couple of halves. I had my lad Louis with me and was talking to a gentleman I'd never seen before. As I was talking with this man, he then uttered, *"Why don't you publish a magazine, Paul?"*

I dismissed the idea. How on earth could I do such a thing? I haven't got a clue of how magazines are published. I would not know where to begin. I went to the men's toilets for a leak. When I returned, the man was gone.

Somehow, it occurred to me that it must be what the Lord wanted me to do. It formed in my mind. Start a magazine. Call it the 'Entertainer'.

"How do I do that?" I asked the Lord in prayer. *"I know nothing about such a thing."* *"Don't worry,"* I seemed to hear back,

and the direction in my mind was clear from somewhere, *"On Monday morning go and talk with the boss man along at Berforts printers at the bottom of London Road in St Leonard's. Talk to him. He will help you."*

I wanted to make sure that I wasn't having delusional after effects from my past shenanigans or that my mind was not playing tricks on me, so I did not tell anyone about what happened.

Later, I understood, that as you speak to Him consistently and form a relationship with Him, in prayers and through reading His word, you become sensitive to His voice, His direction for your life, His visions, and His revelations.

I picked up the good book and read my usual 3 to 4 chapters. I continued my quiet time in prayer, then decided to follow the Lord's direction.

Monday came and I rushed to Berforts printers.

A man answered, *"Hello."* on the intercom. *"I've come to inquire about magazine production,"* I replied.

"Come in," said the man. I was buzzed in. A tall, dark, curly haired chap came down and introduced himself as Vic.

"Hello, Vic, I'm Paul Huggins."

"Yes, I know," replied Vic, "*I followed your boxing career with interest. Pleased to meet you."*

We shook hands. I told him I needed to speak to the owner, the 'boss', about a project that I had in mind.

"Come and sit down," said Vic. *"I'll go and tell him you're here."*

I was shown through to a waiting room that had a very nice tropical fish tank and some comfortable chairs. It wasn't long before the owner came down.

"Hello, I'm Paul."

"I'm Peter," introduced the boss man.

"That's good." I said. *"I'll cut to the chase. I was having a*

word with God last week and he told me to come along and have a chat with you, and that you will help me in my new venture, Sir," I politely finished.

I wasn't sure how Peter would take this information. Perhaps he might patronise me and go ring the local nut house.

"That's very interesting Paul," replied Peter. *"Hang on a mo. I'll just get my wife, Sue."*

I was having a vision that he would return with some men with a straight jacket, but Peter instead, came back with his dear wife, Sue.

"Hello, Paul, pleased to meet you, said Sue. Peter then asked, *"I hope you don't mind me asking, but are you a Christian?"*

"Yes, I am," I replied with pride.

"That's amazing," said Peter. He held his hand out and shook my hand. *"So are we,"* he said, and asked, *"What can we do to help, Paul!?* "

From that day until the Entertainer's last day of publication, Peter Berfort's printing company printed my magazine.

I went away feeling over the moon and thanking my Lord for that amazing blessing that He had given me that day. Nothing short of miraculous.

The Entertainer was to be a free monthly publication.

This is how a free publication works. First, you need to get your price for the number of pages that you want and what size page you will be printing it on. Our magazine would be an A5 magazine with forty-eight pages to start. Peter had given me a good deal. Then, you have to work out how much you will charge for the advertising spaces, and this is obviously how you would make your money.

So many businesses in Hastings have at one time advertised in our magazine and most of the proprietors have become my friends as well.

I wanted a fifty-fifty ratio, that's one-half advertising and the other half with stories etc. to include, a monthly cooking recipe, local up and coming sport events, theatre and music reviews, local history, tide table, book reviews, a what's on out and about guide, and a whole lot more, and of course my own stories. I loved to write, both fact and fiction.

As a massive hand to support me, God sent me a man named Gary Munson, a friend from the Salvation Army.

Gary did the artwork and much of *The Entertainer's* other interesting contents. I had 3 special sections: *the Editorial, the Boxing Review*, where I got to talk about boxing and the *Faith Section*, where I and some guest writers had the space to discuss and explain the Christian faith.

Eventually, after only a few months, the Entertainer magazine was more or less looking after itself. Dave, who I employed in the advertising department was good at selling advertising space. Gary was taking care of the art work. Our story writers and information go-getters did excellently too.

My biggest task each month was to deliver the 5000 copies that were printed.

I was left with time on my hands which I wanted to fill with something practical. An acquaintance of mine, Colin, asked if I would like to be a taxi driver and do some driving for him on weekdays or weekends, hours to suit me. I thought this a great idea. All I needed to do was pass the test of Hastings street knowledge, and have a CRB check, (criminal record bureau) which is a police criminal check to make sure you were safe to work with children and the vulnerable.

I soon had my taxi licence.

I loved driving, and doing it for a living was great fun. It wasn't long before I was nicknamed, 'The Bishop', because I loved talking about my faith and Jesus.

The Entertainer ran for a little over 13 years. Due to other commitments and unforeseen circumstances, I brought the final episode out as a Christmas edition in the year of 2010 in respect of my mother's passing. I thank our Lord that after much persuasion, and prayers, eventually my dear Mother came to church. She accepted the Lord Jesus Christ, and even went along with me to bible study classes.

She was saved when she died.

THE

ENTERTAINER

Issue 76 - April 2004   FREE

Topical Advertiser – 2004 Edition
Covering Hastings, Bexhill, Battle, Rye and other places of interest to you . . .
TELEPHONE: 01424 716834 · E-MAIL: paulhuggins2003@yahoo.com

ENTERTAINER
Topical Advertiser – 2004 Edition

Paul's Diary.

Hallo Peoples,

Here we are in March already. My mum's birthday this month, the first day of spring. Rose, a fitting name to be born on that day. I love this time of year it's a sign of better things to come, buds on the flowers and trees are beginning to sprout and the birds of the wild are beginning to build their nests and the worst of the weather I think has gone... hopefully.

Monday... The Sun is shining. I wish I could say the same; it's been a long celebration having the baby's head 'so to speak' for four months now. It hasn't done me any favours so enough, enough, I'm going to dry out before I forget the real me Ha! Ha! Time to turn on the juice... 'juice', alcohol free and the occasional half.

Tonight I'm going to Kennedy's gym to train and spar with the kids and older lads. Last w did 27 rounds! Over 1½ hours of non-stop boxing. Not bad for 42 coming on 18. We're the A.B.A. officials down soon to register ourselves as a new amateur club. St. Leonard's A.B are to be called, and then when we get our affiliated license we will be in competition with clubs both locally and away. So if you've got some youngsters at home that would like some better to do rather than sit at home and play Nintendo or in some cases watch there paren or get stoned out of their heads (I know, I've been there), send them along to us on a evening. It can only do them the world of good. Even if they don't want to box, they can mix in, and do the training. You will see what a difference it makes in confidence at school. I've seen and been told by parents how their kids are getting on better with a bit of boxing discipline taught to them once or twice a week. Anyway their you go, the offer is there. I'm there from 7pm on Monday's, come and talk to me.

(continued on page 5)

THE BIBLE

The Bible contains 3,566,480 letters, 810,697 words, 31,175 verses, 1,189 chapters, and 66 books. The longest chapter is the 119th Psalm; the shortest and middle chapter, the 117th Psalm. The middle verse is the 8th of the 118th Psalm. The longest name is in the 8th chapter of Isaiah. The word "and" occurs 46,627 times; the word "Lord" 1855 times. The 37th chapter of Isaiah and 19th chapter of the second book of Kings are alike. The longest verse is the 9th of the 8th chapter of Esther; the shortest verse is the 35th of the 11th chapter of John. In the 21st verse of the 7th chapter of Ezra is all the alphabet but "J". The name of our God is not mentioned once in the book of Esther. It contains TRUTH, WISDOM, HOLINESS, and LOVE.

Noa and Brad practising their skills

THE ENTERTAINER March 2004

CHAPTER 28

An investigative journey to the Holy Land

I had lived in my council flat at Egremont Place for too long. I had the property on a mortgage with Hastings council, but because I was away in jail for so long, I owed quite a lot of money.

I decided to make a clean break. My dear friend from King's church, Margaret had a flat in Essenden Rd, St Leonard's-on-sea that was to become empty. I made a deal with Hastings Borough Council Mortgage Department and was soon living in my new cosy little flat with lovely views that went out across the town, then out to sea.

It was just right for me at that time, but I was soon to get itchy feet.

Just then, God had a surprise for me. With some good friends, I had the privilege of visiting the Holy Land in 2006.

For a Christian, Israel connects history and belief. Personally for me, it is not enough for us to believe, but we do have to understand, even to prove, through physical reality, if necessary, what we believe in.

The Bible is historical and true and what better way to find out than visiting the place where the historical events occurred.

Headed by a friend, who was blessed abundantly to finance our entire trip, a group of us, with the goal of searching and uncovering evidence and artifacts to prove the existence of the things and places mentioned in the Bible, we hopped on a plane to the Middle East. Primarily, we wanted to unravel if the Biblical account of Sodom and Gomorrah was true.

There were 8 of us and the plan was to go south to the desert area, to look for the remnants of Sodom and Gomorrah.

Sodom and Gomorrah are two of the cities destroyed by God because of the inhabitants' sinfulness, specifically mentioned in Genesis 19 as: men having sex with other men. The account narrated *"then the Lord rained brimstone and fire on Sodom and Gomorrah"* (Genesis 19:24). The burning sulfur destroyed everything: the buildings, the vegetation, and of course, the people.

We found where the city of Gomorrah was located and searched for brimstones or sulfur samples. Later, we searched and found the city of Sodom as well.

We found some samples after no more than 20 minutes of searching, and briefly after someone in the group prayed.

I was lost for words and in awe because as we searched, we found more and more brimstones.

We collected 68 samples that day and tested them, back in the hotel. They were real. They lit up when we set them alight.

Back in the UK, my friend sent some samples to a laboratory for analysis and they were confirmed to be brimstones.

If thousands of those balls hit you, you would certainly burn to death, and the Lord our God condemned the people in Sodom and Gomorrah, exactly with those brimstones.

The journey to finding Sodom, compared to Gomorrah was a bit difficult. We had to scale a very steep mountain. We almost gave up due to the dangerous terrain until our friend convinced our hired transport to take us as far as the vehicle could go.

Hesitantly, the driver agreed, and we were glad he did because we reached the top.

About 35 kms from Gomorrah, south of the Dead Sea, snuggled between two mountains, was the city of Sodom.

The structures and architecture were still visible with the naked eye. The city, like the remnants of Gomorrah was preserved, though in ruins. The buildings were arranged in terraces. There was a ruin, which looked like a fortress, with doors, windows and walls. There was evidence of temples and even irrigation. It appeared to us as a magnificent city in the past, which, again, was destroyed by God because it turned wicked and evil.

Being in those two significant places reminded us that the judgment of God is real. Of course, God is God, who could do anything. He is also a God who is just and would not hesitate, in His time, to put an end to wickedness.

The next day, we visited many of the sites of the Holy Land, including the place where Jesus was born. We had fun, too, of course. I rode a camel and swam in the Dead Sea.

Walking along the land where Jesus and the disciples actually walked was an altogether amazing experience.

The group in the dessert of Gomorrah.

CHAPTER 29

A calling to India: My first mission

After 7 years in King's church, I felt that God was calling me to another place of worship.

One reason, admittedly, was due to my failed marriage. I lost my temper in one of our arguments and things were blown out of proportion. I tried to restore the relationship, but it was futile. Of course, lessons learned, and through God's grace, I decided to move forward and forget the past.

Even as a Christian, left to my own devices, I struggled with sin, but with genuine repentance and the guidance of the Holy Spirit, I am always brought back to God's grace.

In His Place Community Church, a 15-minute walk from my new flat and headed by a Pastor I knew, Rev. Christopher Sears, he and his wife, Margaret, had done a lot of good for our town, especially for the homeless.

Anyways, that Sunday that I went was special as an Indian Pastor from Hyderabad was visiting. The Indian Pastor spoke and showed us videos of the plight and hardship of the Christian Dalit Children and their families in Hyderabad. The Pastor also told us that there had recently been horrific persecution of Christian families and that they were being tortured and killed in the province of Orissa.

As I listened, I was overwhelmed with sorrow and felt a strong encouraging voice in my head from God, *"Go over and help these children."*

It was confirmed after the service. I was talking to a woman I barely knew, but had seen in church. She said she believed that God wanted me to go and visit the Dalit people in India. I replied,

"Yes, Maam, I believe you are right, it confirms what I have just been thinking too. God wants me to go to India."

On Monday morning, I went to the doctors for a medical checkup and to ask what sort of jabs I would be needing for a trip to India. He took some blood and said he'd be in touch.

I'd sent my passport information to get my Indian visa which arrived back two or three weeks later. I then purchased my 3-month-stay plane ticket to New Delhi airport with the intention of going to just about anywhere in India as the Lord led. I know it sounds so impractical and unrealistic, but I hadn't yet made my mind up where to go once I'd landed. I thought I would ask the Lord for directions when the time came.

A few days after I booked my ticket, I received a phone call from Dr Pandey at the Priory Rd surgery. He asked if I could come and see him that evening. I got to the surgery at 5pm opening time and was asked by the surgery nurse, who was in the waiting room, to go in to Mr. Pandey's office immediately.

After some swift formalities, Dr. Pandey came straight to the point and delivered the shocking news that I was tested positive for aggressive prostate cancer and could have 3 to 5 years to live. Not deterred, I explained, *"But, Doctor, I'm going to India. I have a mission from God to do. I believe He will heal me. I've already bought my ticket to go."*

Dr Pandey looked at me with concern and explained, "But *you won't be able to get medical help if you go to India.*"

Despite his deep-seated concern and reservation, I insisted that I would leave it up to God, and that I had a plane to catch in two weeks' time from Gatwick airport. I then thanked him for his help and added that I would be back in three months.

When I got home, I finally decided to plan and began to search the web for Indian Pastors or missionaries. I came across the name of Pastor Ratan Baboo. After praying about it, I emailed Ratan right there and then and told him that I was a Christian from the UK and that I felt God was calling me to visit him.

The next day I got a reply. Ratan was delighted. We arranged that he would be at the New Delhi airport on my arrival. Two weeks later, I was boarding the plane heading out to New Delhi. 4.177 miles and eight and a half exciting hours later, we touched down.

After the formalities at the immigration, and as planned, there was Pastor Ratan waiting for me at New Delhi airport's arrival exit with a bunch of flowers, just as we had agreed it was how I would recognise him. Thankfully, he was the only man in there with flowers, because there were hundreds of people waiting.

After our informal introduction, we then got a taxi into town. The traffic in India is crazy. I thought Thailand was bad, but here it was constant rush hour all day and most of the nights. Everywhere we stopped, Dalit children would come to the car, and there were all sorts of animals roaming around in the roads.

We found a cheap hostel type building in the back streets of Delhi, where we stayed for the night, before we headed to his home town. Ratan paid the taxi driver. I was too tired to have a full conversation, so we hit the sack.

We were both up bright and early, and we talked over breakfast. Ratan told me that he had a ministry which was way-out somewhere in Assam and was 979 miles away 'as the crow flies'. Ratan went on to say that he and the villagers prayed that someone from somewhere would come and help them out in some small way.

One hour or so later, we were at a train station to board a full day and night train journey to Assam. I assumed that we were heading in the northeastern direction up towards the Himalayas on a train that was huge and powered by a diesel engine. The train was full of all kinds of people, some with animals like chickens and goats. I assume most of them were farmers, and farmers' labourers. There were even people playing musical instruments. There was a continuous flow of train personnel along the carriages with a tray calling out, "*char char.*" We older Brits know it as a nice cup of Char (tea).

The views were magnificent, as far as the eye could see. It soon got dark and so we retired to our hammocks for a night of hectic sleep.

After a long night, we finally arrived at Assam.

I spent a number of weeks with the villagers of Assam, preaching the good news of Jesus Christ, teaching the children, and generally be-friending the locals through my friend and interpreter Ratan. I tried my best with God's guidance to reach out to the Hindu population as well. It was all a wonderful experience and the beginning of my love for the Asian unsaved people.

I was told by Ratan that the British and Americans helped build their railway systems during the Second World War. Of course, India, being a Commonwealth country, has familiar and distinct British architecture too.

I was shown many old railway relics and old steam engines, which were kept in pristine condition.

I also learned of the hardships and terrible persecutions, and worse, the killings of newly converted Christians in Odisha, formally Orissa. I was once again moved to the point that Odisha was my next destination.

So, with the help of Ratan, we got in touch with a Godly man, whom Ratan knew, and arranged that I was to meet him. I was soon on an overnight train and on my way to Odisha with the promise that I would do a fundraising event to help pay for whatever was needed: Bibles, books, etc.

The next day, after a sleepless night on board the train, I finally arrived in the train station at Orissa, where, as arranged by Ratan, I would be met by a man by the name of Dilip Baboo. Apparently, by the way, Dilip is a popular name in India.

The way he was to recognise me was that I was the only white man who would get off the train. How they knew, I did not know.

Indeed, there was Dilip waiting for me in the station and he recognised me immediately because of my skin colour. Dilip was about the same size and build as I was. He was dressed casually in jeans and a light-coloured T-shirt. He had a beaming smile with brilliant white teeth, which looked like they were too large to fit in his mouth, He was delighted to see me, and I was even more delighted because he could speak perfect English.

We then went to his transport which was a 50cc Honda motor bike. We spent the next hour or so driving across country. We passed by rice plantations, fields with Bison roaming around and huge lakes where fishermen were hauling their catch aboard small crafts.

I asked Dilip to stop so that I could have a look at what sort of fish were in the lakes. I found most of the species to be mirror carp of around 10 pounds in weight. I got Dilip to ask the fisherman, who was only a boy, if I could buy one. The lad was so pleased. I purchased a carp for a 200 rupee note, which is about two English pounds.

When we eventually arrived at Dilip's compound, which must have been 40 miles from the nearest town, Dilip introduced me to his wife and the charming orphaned children, whom he and his wife were looking after.

Next, I was shown to where I would be sleeping. It was a rickety old shed with a wooden bed in it that had a hay-filled cloth mattress upon it, and with some goats as my room mates.

I made myself comfortable, then went to see how the fish was being cooked. The fish was cooking wrapped in banana palm leaves on an open fire, along with nans and vegetables of the season. We all had a hearty meal, along with a lengthy discussion on Dilip's mission to help the orphaned children come to know Jesus Christ as their Saviour.

I spent several weeks with Dilip, his wife and his extended family, the orphaned children. We studied and learned together the Word of God. We also played games and even Cricket. I was there in the summer season, when the river, which supplied water to the villagers, dried up. Temperatures soar as high as 48°C, and every day the children would take clay pots and trek for miles to retrieve water from a far off well and then back again. In places such as this and many places around the world, even the basic and simple necessity of water, which we often take for granted, is scarce.

It was a truly eye-opening experience, not only of poverty, but of Dilip and his wife's passion to care for these children and to raise them with the fear of the Lord. Their determination is God given, astounding and admirable, to say the least.

On my return to the UK, I managed to raise some money, as promised, and send it to Dilip via Western Union, but, sadly, I never heard from Dilip again and I wondered what happened. I had done my best at that time. I couldn't bear to think that I had let them down in any way, but I have realised that, in the future, everything has to be carried out, planned, and recorded in an appropriate manner.

Nonetheless, my time in India and with those beloved children were not in vain. My time with Dilip and the children was the birth of the Missionary S.E.E.D, which would be firmly established later in the Philippines.

CHAPTER 30

_____

A new friend in Malta

A week before I was due back into the UK, I was contacted via email by a lady friend, Cath, that I knew from the Old Town of Hastings. It was a pleasant surprise as I didn't know her that well, only that we had talked a couple of times in passing.

I emailed back and explained that I was in India, and would be back in Hastings very soon. She then replied that she was living in Malta. I'd never been to Malta before but I'd seen some magnificent pictures of the place and wondered if there might be a Christian community there. I was in need of a lady companion and was keen to meet up with her. I admitted to her that I had been recently diagnosed with terminal prostate cancer.

I explained though that while I was being prayed for by the Indian children, I had a vision that God was going to use a surgeon to take my prostate cancer away.

Be comforted that if you believe, God heals, even to this day.

Cath was quite impressed and I wondered if this might be the start of a meaningful relationship.

The Operation back home

It wasn't long before I went to see Dr Pandey to tell him that I was back from my missionary trip, and if there was anything that I needed to do in the way of treatment.

He was glad to see me back and immediately arranged with the hospital to have some samples of my prostate snipped off.

The following day, I went to the Conquest Hospital along the Ridge Road in Hastings. The results came back a few days later and the doctor merely confirmed that it was aggressive cancer and that they needed to cut my prostrate out as soon as possible.

I was instructed to go to Eastbourne hospital for the operation just 15 miles along the coast in a westerly direction from Hastings.

A week later, I was booked and led to a private room at the hospital. The room was reserved for paying patients and I wondered why I was in there with my own telly, a fridge and good food being served.

Mr. Destroyer hinted that I was being treated well because it was to be my last few days on the planet.

I later found out that all the other beds were full and that was the only bed, free for me to use. I was grateful that the Lord was taking good care of me. The very pleasant Surgeon came in and told me that I would be having my operation next day, and he reminded me not to eat anything until after the operation. After that, I was given a relaxation pill, and I dozed off until the next morning.

There was no breakfast for me, and it wasn't long before one of the lovely nurses came in and knocked me out. I'd never been knocked out by a woman before, but it was only a little prick in the arm. I was soon out cold in the operation room.

The next thing I knew, I was waking up on the recovery ward and in agony. I cried out to the nurse on duty, *"Nurse! I'm in agony!"*

I made such a fuss, like a big baby. It didn't help that by now the Destroyer kept taunting me inside my head with, *"You're going to die and you're no good to anyone, and you are pathetic and where is your God now?"*

It was so real that I shouted out, *"Away from me! My God is King of Kings and Lord of Lords. He will never leave me nor forsake me. Get away from me Satan, in Jesus' name."*

The nurses heard my shouts and rushed to help me back into my bed, thinking that I was having hallucinations. I was given some strong morphine pain killers, which put me to sleep.

I was kept in the hospital longer than usual for observations. I had a catheter fitted, which collected my urine. I was told that the catheter would be in place for three or four weeks.

Cath turned up to visit. We had a good long talk. I hadn't dated a woman for some time and I needed a companion. So, we agreed that we'd give things a go. I would move over to Malta and could stay with her and her son, Luke, for the time being.

It was no more than two weeks out of Eastbourne hospital and with all my duties and goodbyes taken care of that, along with my catheter and just one suit case of belongings, I landed in Malta.

The year was 2011.

It is now 2021 and I am still alive. The Lord got rid of my cancer through the able hands of the Surgeon and the continuous care of the NHS, just as I believed He would.

Malta

I loved Malta. It is a beautiful holiday destination, rich in history of conquests for thousands of years. First ruled by the Arabs, then by the French when Napoleon Bonaparte took over the Islands from the Knights Templar in 1798, then by the British in the 1800s until 1964.

In 1964, Malta became independent. Being a British colony, they had adopted the English language.

I stayed with Cathy and her son, Luke in the town of Bugibba. Cathy got me a job in the hotel she was working in. I was a kitchen orderly and was washing thousands of dishes a week in this busy holiday destination.

Daily, I was on my hands and knees in pain, scrubbing floors, and while manual labour is not exactly new to me, I found this one really tough. Certainly, another good lesson on humility.

I found a good Bible believing church not too far away in Gzira. The church is called Bible Baptist Church which was founded by Joseph Mifsud and his wife, Jenny. Joe and his, wife, Jenny work tirelessly to spread the Word of God. We went on the streets and just about everywhere, delivering tracts.

Cathy came with me when she wasn't working and, hopefully, seeds were planted. Sadly, things didn't work out the way we would have both wanted. And after a few months, I began to think that Malta, as beautiful as it is, was too small for me. I felt like a big elephant in a small circus. I wanted to escape and be somewhere where I could be more useful in the big wide world. I also realised that, perhaps, I rushed into the relationship and I should be looking for a Christian woman, who shares my faith and who I can work with in the service of God.

It was not a relationship which God intends to be, in the first place. I was so longing for a woman companion, that I did not care if I disobeyed Him. God's intention is for a man and a woman to be wed, and to live together as a husband and wife. For Christians, it also meant to be yoked with other Christians in marriage.

Someone at church told me about a Christian website where you could register for free and build a profile with your picture and then search for other Christian singles. I began talking with a Christian lady from Wales, and we got on really well.

It was so promising that I proposed to her and even met her family in Switzerland, but that sadly was also not meant to be.

I found myself, once again, alone and wanting.

Obviously, God had other plans for me and, because of my love for the Asian people, it came to mind that was the place to look for the future love of my life.

Meanwhile, after a year of returning to Hastings, the job in a hotel in Malta inspired me to take up courses and obtain a diploma in Hospitality, Catering and Food Hygiene in Sussex Coast College.

CHAPTER 31

My dream came true

We have an old saying in the Old Town, *'A woman will draw you further than gunpowder will blow you.'*

So, back on the web, I searched for a lady in Asia and trusted that God was going to give me the lady of my dreams. I refer literally, to a dream I had so many years ago. In my dream, the love of my life looked Asian and I saw her from a distance, walking in a garden in a red dress. That dream, literally, came true.

An online search for a girlfriend was not the norm for me. Compared to how things are in the non-Christian environment, especially in pubs, finding a girlfriend is relatively easy. But finding a Christian girlfriend, in my experience, was like finding a needle in a haystack. But I was relentless.

There was no way that I could stay single for the rest of my life and so this was the only way to find a bride as far as I was concerned. So, from my little bedsit in Newport, Wales, I searched for a Christian lady from Asia. After all, I'd been to Asia on the understanding that was the place God wanted me to be. I had a feeling I was about to begin yet another amazing journey.

The world wide web could be a wonderful thing in many ways if used wisely.

As I scrolled through literally hundreds of beautiful, single Asian Christian women who were looking for a handsome western Christian husband like me, I came across a lovely looking lady by the name of Bernadette.

"Stop!" said a gentle voice in my head. So I did and continued to read all about Bernadette, which was very impressive. Bernadette was a practising Barrister in the Philippines, who lived in Manila her profile stated.

I sent Berns an email sharing my testimony of faith in our Lord, hoping that I would hear back from her soon. And soon enough, we were having a lovely to and fro conversation for a couple of months until we decided that our meeting together, albeit online, was an act of God. We prayed a lot too together during those times.

I decided that I would have to be on the plane to Manila airport as soon as possible. That night, I prayed to our Lord and thanked Him for giving me Berns and yet another chance to start a new life, possibly in Asia, with the hope of carrying out the great commission.

As Christians, we all have the duty and were commissioned to share the Good News of salvation in Jesus (Matthew 28:18-20): *"And Jesus came and spoke to them, saying. 'All authority has been given to Me in heaven and on earth. Go therefore and make disciples of all the nations, baptizing them in the name of the Father and of the Son and of the Holy Spirit, teaching them to observe all things that I have commanded you; and lo, I am with you always, even to the end of the age.' Amen.*

A couple of months later, I was back in Hastings, staying with my brother, Dean, for a few days. Then I was on the plane approaching Manila airport with all my worldly possessions packed into a suitcase.

On arrival at Manila International Airport, Berns was waiting for me with a big smile and a warm hug. She told me that I looked better in person. Berns was shorter than I had anticipated but I was delighted with what I saw in the flesh. We hit it off straight away. She told me that Ton-Ton, Berns' personal driver, was waiting for us in the Arrivals car park.

By the time we got to the car, it was as though I'd known Berns all my life. Sure enough, there was Ton-Ton waiting in a white car. He got out from the car to help me with my case. Ton-Ton, who was dressed casually, was a chubby, jovial chap, an inch or two taller than me who could communicate well in the English language.

Our first stop was at Rainbow Ridge, thirty minutes away from the airport. Berns lived in a private condominium (a flat in a block) with a large wrought iron entrance gate manned by an armed guard which was typical in Manila

Berns had arranged for me to stay at a flat above hers, which a friend owned, but who was on a long vacation.

I soon met Berns' Dad, Papa Rico, who was in his early 60s, and her Mum, Betty, her sisters, RJ and Princess, brother Frederick and her adorable nephews and nieces, who speak English like native speakers. They lived in the province of Batangas, 2 hours away, south of Manila.

Papa resembled a Mexican gangster sporting a handsome moustache. My father-in-law was retired from working in the Libyan and Oman's oil fields, and was fortunate to enable his children to attend private schools and universities.

Papa Rico was one of the founder members of MCJC Mediterranean Church of Jesus Christ, which originated in Libya and now had chapters in Taguig, Luzon and Antipolo City of the Philippines. He became a Believer and a Born-Again-Christian in Libya and told me that he used to frequent Malta as well.

After retirement, he established a family business, a pharmacy and operates a market place. He continues to preach the Gospels to all who would listen. By God's grace, his prayers and perseverance, most of his family have converted from the Catholic religion to the born-again Christian faith.

Religion cannot and does not save. Faith is found and deepened in a personal relationship with our Lord Jesus, who makes us new.

As it is written in the Scripture, *Jesus said "Truly, truly, I say to you, unless one is born again, he cannot see the kingdom of God."* (John 3: 3)

The wedding and the birth of a ministry

There was much excitement in the Esguerra family prior to our wedding on the 14th of September 2015. Filipinos love their families and are very clannish.

I met some of Berns' family in Batangas and to say that Filipinos love food, much to my full satisfaction, is an understatement. Wherever we were invited, there would be a feast of a scrumptious mix of Filipino and continental spread.

The wedding itself was the fruit of God's provisions. Berns' family and friends from Victory church helped her in the preparations. We had 50 or so guests on our invitation list and so it was arranged that we would be married in a historic beautiful building that housed a very popular restaurant in the city of Manila.

We were married by Pastor Jonathan Camcam who is one of the Pastors of Victory Church. Berns looked stunning in her beautiful gown and I in my Barong, which is the Filipino national costume for special events. The wedding reception took place in the same area where the wedding was held. There was a spit roast pig, donated by one of our wedding sponsors, Ethel, and a buffet table filled with mouthwatering Filipino food. We had a stringed quartet who played popular classic and contemporary music to the delight of the well-fed guests. In all, it was a very memorable afternoon.

We then said our goodbyes under a rain of confetti, then headed off towards our honeymoon destination to Baguio, which took us 6 hours by bus. Baguio is the coolest part of the Philippines because it is way up in the mountains.

It was during our honeymoon where I saw Berns as the woman in my dreams. We were in a tourist destination, in a garden, and she wore a red dress. As I watched her from a distance, walking towards me, it suddenly occurred to me that this was 'my dream', decades ago.

We enjoyed a lovely week together exploring the city, then made our way back to Taguig to Rainbow Ridge, where we lived.

With Pastor Jonathan in our wedding.

Honeymoon in Baguio.

One month after we were married, we began our ministry, the Missionary S.E.E.D., with its roots now firmly planted in the Church at Antipolo City, just over 14 miles away from our flat in Rainbow Ridge, Taguig.

This organization was officially registered with the Securities and Exchange Commission (SEC. REG. No CN201523880) on December 7, 2015 as an affiliate of The Mediterranean Church of Jesus Christ in Antipolo, with the primary purpose of Supporting, Educating, Equipping and Developing the children in the impoverished area of Antipolo City. We are guided by this Biblical verse in Proverbs 22:6: *"Train up a child in a way he should go. And when he is old, he will not depart from it"*.

From then on, every Sunday, my father-in-law Pastor Rico would pick us up for the trip to our church MCJC in Antipolo City that he pastored along with Pastor Zak and Pastor Willy. The church was only half built, then, but at least it had a roof to protect us whenever the rains came falling. It had considerably been improved since we left.

Initially, there were around 70 children, 4 to 15 years of age, who regularly attended S.E.E.D. We conducted activities like Bible lessons, group discussions, games, sports, singing, and film showing. We also fed the children, and they looked forward to the food a lot, understandably.

These activities were all possible through the help of our team of excellent and committed volunteers from the church: Sister Dorina, Sister Susan, Sister Nemia, Rhea, Marianne, Rechelle, and many others. Along with Berns, they take care of the children's ministry, teaching and preparing the food.

From time to time, we also conducted tutorials for the children. We have a programme called *'Adopt a scholar: bridging the gap, spreading the love'*. Sponsorships from the Philippines and the UK help make this programme possible. To date, there are 25 scholars benefitting from this scholarship program.

A group picture, taken in our early days of S.E.E.D.

Our first year of S.E.E.D. was remarkable and God used individual sponsors and organizations to bless us. We were a recipient of goods (food, toys, clothes, etc.) from Real Life Foundation, the scholarship arm of Victory Fort, Philippines. We handed the donations to the community and the children we served in December, 2015 and in 2016. We conducted a medical mission in March, 2016, sponsored by an international NGO, Remote Area Medical. The medical mission paved the way for the impending needed surgeries of three of our S.E.E.D. children suffering from various illnesses and defects. An artist from the UK, Christina Cassisa, in cooperation with West Hill Boxing Club, and my friends, Mick Hammer, Mick Turner, Paul Crimin, Mark Dockerell, etc. also led a fund-raising activity, which managed to raise 300 pounds.

Also, beginning July 2016 and one hour before the Sunday S.E.E.D. activities, a Korean Pastor and his team from Living Water Church in Taytay, Rizal, had started giving the children lessons on musical instruments like flute, recorder, xylophone, drums, etc.

A regular Sunday afternoon in S.E.E.D.

Intercom Media Resources from the US also sent us 50 DVDs on Christianity, which was very useful to our goal to disciple the children.

In 2017, David Fuller of Fuller Engineering, sent us a crate full of all kinds of goods, which we distributed to the children and their families. It was the biggest donation we had received, to the great delight of the children and their families.

An individual sponsor, who later became a much-loved friend and an adopted grandmother to Berns, Hazel Ruddle, also gave us funds monthly in support of our weekly activities. Sadly, Grandma Hazel passed away in early 2021. Filipino friends of Berns in the Philippines and from other parts of the world donated school supplies and Christmas lunches every year.

Reflecting back, as I walked around from house to house in the slum area of Antipolo, I was always very emotional. Similar to India, there were kids of all ages running around with nothing on their feet. They live with their struggling-to-survive parents in made up shanty structures of tin sheets nailed to flimsy wooden beams with no floors. Their cooking facilities were made of concrete blocks with, if they were fortunate enough, a calor gas bottle. Either that or wood burners.

Some eked out a living from selling coffee or ice cream or fruit and vegetables from trollies, which were pushed around the slums, or by stitching baseball sportswear for as little as 2 pounds a day.

It was no surprise that the kids initially looked forward to going to Sunday school because of the food we serve.

It is estimated that over 20 million people live in slum areas of the Philippines with tens of thousands of those living near our church.

You can view some short amateur videos, which we have made from our MCJC church in Antipolo City, on our YouTube channel: the Missionary S.E.E.D. Some of the videos showed the harsh conditions of children's lives. The videos were made during 2016 and those kids are now grown up. Most have moved to Secondary Education. More importantly, most have decided to follow Jesus and, by His grace, have been transformed in confidence and good character.

Incidentally, proceeds of this book will go towards the ministry as it is ongoing, and we do have plans, as God WILLS it, of replicating it in some ways in Hastings.

Marrying Berns and running S.E.E.D. gave me a meaningful purpose in life. Like any marriage, ours could be turbulent but through S.E.E.D. it is also productive and mission oriented.

After a year, we realised how different we were. She is an academic and an intellectual who sometimes lacks common sense, and I am street smart, who at times cannot spell a word or two. I do not understand her world of law and she does not know anything about boxing. She loves rice. I can eat potatoes for life. She is organised, and I could be all over the place. She loves to plan while I am spontaneous and a risk-taker, to say the least. She does not appreciate alcohol at all. I like a drink or two occasionally. I am careful with money, and she can give away everything she has. While coming from completely opposite backgrounds and culture, we also discovered that we share a love for the simple things in life, like food, nature, even writing and politics. More importantly, that we can forget and forgive our differences, and choose to love and to work well together.

Berns told me that before meeting me she prayed hard for a man who she could partner with in serving the Lord. She even called it a mission together. She did not know yet that several years ago in India, I had begun the Missionary S.E.E.D.. God knows, I needed a reliable partner to keep the organization going, and God answered both of our prayers.

Indeed, God answers the prayers of His children according to His will, specifically if it is for His purposes.

A journey back to Hastings

Life in the Philippines, though fruitful in the Lord's work, was quite complicated for me. I could not find employment. People, while friendly, were not used to my accent. The Philippines were also colonised by the Americans and so Americanised. While the majority could speak English, they were not used to a British twang and often were stunned by how I spoke.

Berns worked during the week in her office in Manila and I would walk around talking with the locals who might speak English and generally tried to make friends to be able to witness my faith.

The highlight of my week was Sunday Church and S.E.E.D. On some days, I would write this book. I also found an Online Resource, which kept my brain active and enabled me to finish a complete Bible course. I love defending my faith and so I needed equipping.

Sensing my feelings of isolation and homesickness, which living in a foreign country naturally brings, Berns asked if I wanted to visit England for a while. I did not hesitate. Thankfully, and what would be the beginning of a restored relationship, I asked my Dad and Stepmum, Diane, for a ticket back home. They gladly paid for my plane fare.

With my wife at Canterbury.

My journey back to Hastings was once again a miracle of God's provisions. What initially was just a visit, turned into a plan of moving back home with Berns. But to make it happen, I would be needing a place to stay, a job and the proof of an annual income of £18,600, as per the Home Office requirements. I connected with one of my cousins, Dave, through Facebook and asked if he knew of possible employment for me. He directed me to Barry Coleman, who gave me a job even before moving back to Hastings. Next, was a place to stay and it was provided through my long time Christian friend, Keith William Wright. Keith did not hesitate to 'house me' for a while.

I arrived in Hastings in April of 2017, stayed with Keith in his house, worked at Coleman Construction and became a member of a no-nonsense Bible-based Evangelical church, Emmanuel.

Being a part of the church is important for fellowship and spiritual growth. The church is a big blessing, as the congregation prayed for Berns to be granted a spouse visa. The spouse visa, to enable me to get Berns into the country, was not an easy process, with lots of documentary requirements. While most people use Solicitors, Keith, who had some experience with an application, assisted us from beginning to end. I had to work overtime most days and weeks to meet the financial requirement.

God provided for everything we needed, including certifications and recommendations from a friend, tax consultant and Tackleway Football Team Manager, Mick Southon, our Reverend in Emmanuel Church, Martin Lane, and Berns' friends from the Philippines.

Living apart from my wife was tough. I missed her a lot.

By God's grace, our visa was granted in July of 2018, and one month after, Berns flew to the UK to be with me. She wanted to see London and catch up with some of her cousins there. So dear friends of ours, Margie and Adrian, who lived near

Heathrow, picked her up from the airport.

Our first year in Hastings was marred with adjustments and conflicts. Surely, no relationship is free of conflict but thanks be to God, Berns and I have learned to face life and its unexpected circumstances with wisdom, peace and joy in the Lord.

It has been 2 years and a half since Berns came over and a lot has happened, including the COVID pandemic.

In October, 2019, Berns and I acted together in our first play called *Just Desserts*, staged by SHADES, a Christian, Amateur, Evangelisitic Threatre Company, whose mission is to share the Gospel through drama and sketches. One of the founders, David Henty, invited us to join and eventually we were acting ourselves. We both enjoyed acting, though I was often frustrated with myself for my inability to memorise lines, but we got there in the end.

Last Christmas 2020, I even played Angel Gabriel.

Unconvinced? Here is a photo taken with the other members of the cast at His Place Community Church:

We also joined a writing group called Shorelink, because I wanted to improve my writing. The members all encouraged me to just write, keep on writing and it would get done eventually. They were right.

We continue to support S.E.E.D., albeit overseas, and to attend Emmanuel Church, which is a 5-minute walk from where we live along Emmanuel Road in Hastings.

Whenever opportunity arises, we witness for the Lord. As I said in the beginning of this book, I have never been, and would never be, ashamed of my faith, because it has saved me and it would save you too.

Last year, due to the pandemic, I lost my job for a couple of months but God provided, as He always does. The provision was through a friend, Alan Marchant, whom I had not seen for what must have been a decade.

After a few months of meeting him again, I began working on his farm.

Since I had not touched base with Alan for years, I could only describe our reunion as divine. Time and again, God was at work in all these things.

I was looking for a water-proof jacket and decided to visit a shop in town, which Alan once owned. After a brief conversation with the new owner, I realised that Alan had sold the shop to her. She added that Alan is engaged with the love of his life, Juliet. He is happily retired, tending his farm, and alcohol free. She gave me Alan's number. Alan was both elated and stunned to hear from me.

He did not know where I was and he even assumed I had died from cancer. Later, we would meet when he came to see our play, '*Just Desserts*'. I found out he wrote about me in his book, 'A Drunkard's Nightmare: An End to a Living Hell'.

* * *

"Even more sadness was on its way. Paul, my soul mate through all this, was diagnosed with cancer. I cannot tell you how bad this affected me. The man that I honestly believe was sent to me by my Saviour was now dying himself. The following months were very hard to swallow and to this day it brings tears to my eyes. We would talk or laugh or cry together and I could not understand why he was ill. It felt like a dream, but it was becoming a very real one, and it had a deep emotional effect on me."

* * *

(at page 33)

Alan was an alcoholic, like I had been. I met him when I was driving taxis. He often called me in his drunken state to be driven home, or to get some cans from the off licence for him.

Knowing that Jesus was the only way for him to sober up, I began inviting him to church, and continuously encouraged him that there is hope to be found only in Jesus.

And indeed, with praises to Jesus, Alan, in his own words, had a divine encounter with the ultimate Saviour, who gave him the courage and strength to give up alcohol altogether.

WHAT NOW? Well, here come the lessons

CHAPTER 32

The lessons of my life from being a child of the devil to a child of God

I have told you my story from beginning to end. There are many more stories in between, but my story, like that of so many others who have accepted Jesus, is a story of transformation. I have been, by the grace of God, transformed from a child of the devil to now a child of God.

From my early days as a Christian, I have admitted that I struggled for years. When I drank, I would drink excessively. I continued to smoke weed, I swore a lot, I even looked at porn on occasions and I slept with a number of women out of wedlock. As mentioned, I also had a failed marriage.

But I am a work in progress.

Through Jesus and the Holy Spirit, I continue to KNOCK OUT MY DEMONS on a daily basis.

Let it be stressed that I am far from perfect and holy but certainly I am no longer the person I used to be in so many substantial ways.

Whenever I fail, He brings me back to Him. Most encouraging is that I can rely on His promise that He will bring to completion, the work He had begun in me (Philippians 1:6).

I could not deny, from the number of occasions of my near-death experiences, that I often wondered why I was kept alive.

In retrospect, one of the good reasons from being saved literally and figuratively is that I have the privilege of telling you my story and sharing with you the 10 most important lessons I have learned in my life of almost 60 years, **I'm crying out to you**:

1. Evil pursues sinners; and so please get to know Jesus

You might have wondered why it took me so long to change, despite being fully aware of the damages my behaviour caused, not only to myself, but to my family, friends, and society in general. As mentioned, it is because we cannot change ourselves, no matter how much we try.

Evil also pursues sinners. I referred to the Evil One as Mr. Destroyer in this book. And that is exactly what he intends to do, destroy lives, and our whole being. It hardens and eliminates conscience. All the devil wants to do as is written in God's word is, *"The thief does not come except to steal, to kill and to destroy. I have come that they may have life and that they may have it more abundantly."* (John 10:10)

Evil could overcome and overpower us, like it did to me. You might think that you have not committed any of the crimes I have committed, or could never do any of the things I did.

Well, let me put a stop to your assumption? We all have the same problem of sin and we are all spiritually dead, unless we repent of our sins. Your misdemeanors might not exactly be as grave as mine but sin is sin. Lying is sin. Gossiping and bad-mouthing your neighbour are sins. Even looking at a man or a woman with lust is a sin. The bible says, *"For all have sinned and fall short of the glory of God."* (Romans 3:23).

Meanwhile, because I was totally under the direction of the Evil One, and helplessly and willingly participating in his wicked manoeuverings, I could not change myself. However, when my eyes, mind and heart were opened to faith in Jesus through the Bible, and as guided by the Holy Spirit the direction of my life slowly changed. Jesus saved me from myself and from Mr. Destroyer.

Jesus gave me a new heart, which allowed me to have a personal relationship with Him. This is what it means to be born again. Through the Bible, He taught me how to live a better life. *"Therefore, if anyone is in Christ, he is a new creation: the old has gone, the new has come!"* (2 Corinthians 5:17).

This leads me to the most important lesson I would like to share: If you do not want to die and go to hell, get to know Jesus through the Bible.

Our greatest failure in life would be to reject our Creator and His son, Jesus Christ, who died to save us from the penalty of our sins. Rejecting God and Jesus lead to death, and the kind that is eternal. The eternal damnation in hell.

My wife and I loved to say that if you have to put your faith in something, put it in your Creator and in Jesus. The epilogue of this book will touch briefly on this.

Repenting of my sins, accepting Jesus and what He had done for me is the best thing that happened in my life. My faith is my greatest blessing.

We cannot save ourselves from continuous sinning, and from the penalty of our sins, but Jesus had done it for us on the cross. Please understand that we do not need to do anything except to believe and repent and we will be saved. Salvation is faith in what Jesus had done for us on the cross. Certainly, we cannot pay for our sins in the way that Jesus had, though He never sinned.

We cannot earn our way to heaven through our own merits, efforts, and good works. It is only through God's grace. Everything is through His grace, so that no one can boast. *"For it is by grace you have been saved, through faith – and this not from yourselves, it is the gift of God – not by works, so that no one can boast."* (Ephesians 2: 8-9).

2. Discipline your children promptly and appropriately with love

In the first part of this book, I mentioned about the light admonitions I received, early as a child. A light admonition from stealing from my mum's purse. A light admonition which somehow created the impression that I could get away with doing wrong, especially if it is for a good cause.

Disciplining promptly and appropriately, with love, is the key to correcting the bad behaviour of our children. Anything we do creates an impression and leaves a mark.

It is a must to discipline your child, especially if you see that your child is doing the wrong things. If you need to ground your child, then do it. Discipline, remind them that there will always be consequences to their actions and that they could be punished for their wrong doing. It also creates fear and reverence.

Even the bible encourages us to take action with the following verses from Proverbs:

Proverbs 13:24: *He who spares the rod hates his son, but he who loves him disciplines him diligently.*

Proverbs 19:18: *Discipline your son, for in that there is hope; do not be party to his death.*

Proverbs 23:12: *Apply your heart to instruction and your ears to words of knowledge.*

God calls you to take action, specifically when your children are misbehaving.

My childhood experience is also the reason why I and my wife have established the Missionary S.E.E.D. I wanted to impart the Christian values, which I lacked as a child, to kids, especially the underprivileged.

God willing, we will be able to establish one here in Hastings soon.

3. Value what lasts, and appreciate what you have

Values are crucial. They define us and our lives. I have learned that valuing the wrong things (money, fame, ourselves, our pleasures, our own happiness) leads to nothing and to an endless pursuit of things that do not last.

On the other hand, valuing what lasts, such as our personal relationships, our God- given talents, learning things, pursuing a valuable trade or employment and helping people, gives meaning to our lives. It is important to define our values early on in life. It is important to know what truly matters in life, or we would be easily swayed and enticed by the values which the world offers.

I did not know what was truly valuable early in life, and I lived most of my life valuing the wrong things. I had no idea that what is valuable cannot be bought. I did not know that what is valuable is in the Bible and within reach.

And because I valued the wrong things, I also did not appreciate what I had until they were all gone. For example, I did not realise how valuable getting a good education was, or, at least, seriously learning a trade, until I struggled in my job hunting. I often tell myself, "If only I knew then what I know now, I would have studied harder or put more effort into my classes . . ."

It's the same situation with boxing. I knew that boxing, like most sports, is not a long-term career, but I did not care. It was gone before I had a chance to truly appreciate it for what it's worth.

When you're young, it seems that everything could last forever but it won't.

So, value what lasts, stay true to your values and appreciate what you have.

4. I am not the epicentre of the universe.

I used to think that the world revolved around me. When people adore you, it's easy to fall into the pits of self-importance and vanity. Undoubtedly, too, I was utterly selfish and everything in life was all about me and myself.

But slowly, when I become a Christian, and began learning about the world God created, I realised how tiny I was, not necessarily insignificant, but I was small, literally and figuratively, compared to the beautiful world He has created.

We are not the epicentre of the universe. I think paying as much attention to what is happening around us, and how what we do affects other people, would help to keep things in perspective. It's very difficult to view the world from a perspective outside of your own. It is harder to see and understand the world when we are too focused on ourselves, and our lives. For instance, now I know how drugs truly destroy society in general, and how poverty affects hundreds of millions of people around the world.

In the bigger scheme of things, the world does not revolve around us and it should not. I am still struggling with my self-importance, but the Holy Spirit continues to work in me, to remind me of who I am in Christ. My wife is often quick to remind me to keep my feet on the ground. She cringes when I boast of anything, and rightly so.

Thinking deeply, my vanity might have been due to my deep-seated insecurities, but we all need genuine humility. Again, genuine humility we cannot have and gain without the power of God's grace and transformation. God alone can equip us with the strength to do what is right, and to behave accordingly.

Apart from Him, we are nothing, and we cannot do anything.

Everything is little compared to God. God is what matters in my story. In Psalm 56:8, David wrote, "*You number my wandering;*

put my tears in Your bottle. Are they not in Your book?"
In Psalm 139:13–14 he says, *"For You formed my inward parts;*
You knitted me together in my mother's womb. I praise You, for I
am fearfully and wonderfully made. Wonderful are Your works; my
soul knows it very well."

5. The Love of Money is the Root of All Evil

This is a verse found in 1 Timothy 6:10: *For the love of money is a*
root of all kinds of evil.

And this is certainly true for me. I loved money. I loved what
it bought me. I loved money too much that it led me to my criminal
activities.

Please note that the Bible qualified the verse, so that it is the
LOVE of money and not money, per se, which is the root of all evil.

Money is a tool, a commodity that buys you the necessities
in life and so money is essential.

However, when you love it too much, then you must watch
yourself. Remind yourself that while money can give you some
comforts, and even a bit of security, it cannot give you long-lasting
happiness. Money does not guarantee you a wonderful life, and
definitely not a free-from-problem life. It cannot cure your loneliness,
nor can it make you feel better about yourself.

More importantly, pure satisfaction in material gains that
money buys could lead you to forget God and His grace.

6. Natural talent is nurtured with focus and total commitment

I was given a natural ability to box, but to be good at something
requires hard work, focus and total commitment. I worked hard
during my boxing career but I lacked total focus and commitment.
As you have read, I led a double life.

Truly, not giving boxing my total commitment by engaging in
the pursuit of my pleasures along with it, is regretful. I regretted

not giving my hometown, Hastings, the coveted professional boxing championship it deserved.

Of course, I also failed to honour God's given ability when I did not focus. I did not know that, of course, but that is the lesson. God gives us talents and it is up to us to nurture them and be a good steward of what He gives us.

Boxing was meant to give me discipline but I had other things in mind, which got in the way.

If you are an athlete, treasure your talent and ability. Nurture them, because taking action is critical. Working towards your goals to the top and making plans for the future is commendable and often very useful.

But I also learned that you do not need to rush at full speed at anything. Take your time too, and its okay to slow down.

7. Relationships require selfless love and effort

God created us to be relational. We are not meant and not created to be alone. He created Adam and Eve. He knew Adam needed Eve, and Eve, Adam. He knew we need our fellow humans to survive.

In the past, I did not really value my personal relationships because of my selfishness and my lack of sense. Now I know better. Relationships require selfless love and effort. Selfless love is what God requires and, practically, it is what is needed. Jesus gave that love. It was selfless. He died on the cross, so we could live. And God's love is unconditional, so that even if we fail Him, He would bring us back, if we are willing to receive. John 3:16-17 says," *For God so loved the world, that He gave his only begotten Son, that whosoever believeth in Him should not perish, but have everlasting life. For God sent not his Son into the world to condemn the world; but that the world through him might be saved.*"

That kind of love is not humanly possible.

If we remind ourselves that God chose to love us, and is willing to save us, even if we fail and do not deserve His forgiveness, it would be easy to choose to let annoyances pass, to be faithful, to be kind and to just choose to love.

8. In this life, we would have troubles, but often we bring the troubles to our own lives

No life is easy. In fact, sometimes, it is downright painful, is it not? We all have our fair share of struggles on different levels.

The absolute truth is that in this life we will have troubles. Even a Christian is not spared from troubles. The Bible is clear on that, because Jesus had troubles and experienced the most agonizing death on the cross, but He overcame. *"These things I have spoken to you, that in Me you may have peace. In the world you will have tribulation; but be of good cheer, I have overcome the world."* (John 16:33).

While we all are not immune to troubles, my life is also a testimony, that we could bring our own troubles to our own lives through our wrong choices, blatant rejection of God and what is good. While we naturally struggle in life, we should also be fully aware that sometimes our struggles might be the result of our own doing.

But life's troubles have good purposes, even for an unbeliever or someone who does not have faith in God and in Jesus.

I had to fail, many, many times, and had to experience total hopelessness before I was directed to the right path through God's grace.

God did it for me and He can do it for you too. He loves you just the same, He wants you back and He wants the best for you.

Thankfully, the solution to our life's troubles is within our reach and He is ready and willing to do the impossible for us, if we let Him.

9. We all mess up but God can turn things around, if we let Him

We all have visions of our ideal life. We all have dreams. We all want the best for our children.

But sometimes our dreams fail. Sometimes, like I did, we mess up. I have done foolish and wicked things and have suffered the often bitter consequences of my own actions. But God arranged things in my life to fulfill His purpose of transformation. It is beyond understanding but while we cannot understand His ways (Isaiah 55;9), we can trust Him.

The truth is we all mess up but it does not mean that we should live and stay messed up.

What God did for me He can do for you. He is good. If you let Him, He can change you. He would give you a second, a third chance even, until you are redeemed and fully His.

He would cleanse you of your sins, of your mistakes and make you new and whole again. He alone has the power to transform us.

The better news is that He will not condemn you of your past. Society might, but your Creator would never condemn you.

And the best news is if you become His child, He will not leave you as you are. He will transform you through and through. Being a Christian does not mean perfection but He promises to sanctify us until we are as white as snow.

He would also provide you with everything you need to do good things for Him.

You would not lack, because He would provide for your needs.

He promised He would be your refuge in times of trouble,

He is trustworthy and His promises are true.

And, most importantly, you would experience a love like no other.

10. God is in control, not us

God is in ultimate control of the world He has created. He is in charge. He is sovereign. He is in control of every little thing that happens in this world. He sustains it hour by hour, day by day.

Before I became a Christian, I, under the direction of the Devill, took control of my life. I could not resist the Devil but then miraculously God gave me a choice. When I chose Him, I realised that ultimately, He is the one in charge.

When I became a Christian, I understood God's sovereignty and power in meaningful ways. As I have written here, I have experienced how He causes things to happen in my life. He makes the impossible, possible. He provides the way and He is the way.

He has the power to turn the adversity and painful circumstances that happen in our lives around for our good.

So, if you think you are in control, it is an illusion because He is. As mentioned, throughout my Christian life, I witnessed how God took care of even the mundane details in my life. He is connected and concerned with the lives of His people.

RESOURCES

The Bible

If you have not yet believed in Jesus, and have reached the end of this book, I encourage you to look up for yourself all the verses from the Bible, which I have quoted. The Bible is the living Word of God and I urge you to please get yourself one. As I have testified in this book, it was the Bible, as guided by the Holy Spirit, which brought me to faith in Jesus.

God speaks to us through the Bible. It is His History, our History, our Present, our Future. It is the Perfect Book, which guides us, directs us and gives us purpose, meaning and joy.

The Apostle Paul described in 2 Timothy 3:16, *"All Scripture is given by inspiration of God, and is profitable for doctrine, for reproof, for correction, for instruction in righteousness."*

Learning more about creation

The Bible teaches us that God created the world and that it did not come about from a big, empty hole. It also teaches us that He created us, both men and women, and that we did not evolve from monkeys, as Charles Darwin would make us believe in his evolution theory.

We all have a world view of how the world was created and who created it, regardless of the evidence. Our views are very important, as it would eventually define what we believe, and even how we live.

I found that scientists who are not Christians will try and tell us their theories of how the universe came into being ranging from an explosion from nothing to unobservable theories.

However, everything, plain to sight, points to an incredible designer and science can confirm the existence of God. There are the Christian scientist believers who, after rigorous study and observations, have come to faith in our creator God because of the overwhelming evidence that it is impossible to come from nothing, from an explosion of chaos. Just to name a few: Professor Dr Dean Kenyon, who was a biochemical evolutionist, now Christian; atheist Astrologer and Physicist Huge Ross, Dr Patrick Briney, a committed evolutionist atheist, now both Christians and the famous Ph.D. Dr of Microbiology, the German genius, Professor Gunther Scheizle; and last, but not the least, Professor of Physics, Isaac Newton.

Someone once said that Darwinian evolution is a theory that will tell us more and more about less and less until we know everything about nothing.

If you care to look deeply, there is a very interesting YouTube channel called Origins Cornerstone TV, which discusses the scientific evidence behind Creation and the Creator.

The Church

What better way to find out more about our God, and the saving grace of our Lord, Jesus Christ than through a church.

I am encouraging you to look for a church in your area, which teaches the Word of God faithfully. Not all churches do and not all churches are the same but let me caution you that no church is perfect.

A good church provides not only sound teaching of the Bible but fellowship with other believers, who would welcome you and encourage you to grow in faith. Belonging to a good church means an extended family, too, and we all need one. It is called a spiritual family, because we belong to one Father in Heaven.

As mentioned, we belong to such a church called Emmanuel Church, located along Vicarage Road in Hastings. More information can be found in http://www.emmanuelhastings.org.uk/ . If you live nearby, you are welcome to come and join us on Sundays.

EPILOGUE

As I continue to KNOCK OUT MY DEMONS, I keep on fighting, but now God is my Cornerman, Jesus is my Referee and the Holy Spirit, my counselor and my cheerer.

With God, I can't lose and I won't lose.

I am also confident of where I would be, when life's final bell rings.

You can fight well, too, if you choose to fight with Jesus.

"I have fought the good fight. I have finished the race. I have kept the faith.

Finally, there is laid up for me the crown of righteousness, which the Lord the righteous Judge will give to me on that day, and not to me only, but also to all who have loved His appearing." (2 Timothy 4:7-8)

As I end this book, it is my hope and prayer that you who are without faith will know Jesus. I will continue to pray that God will reveal the truth to you like He has done for me.

"And you shall know the truth and the truth shall set you free." (John 8:32)

And as the song goes by John Newton.

Amazing grace! How sweet the sound
That saved a wretch like me;
I once was lost, but now am found,
Was blind, but now I see.

And He will save you to if you truely believe. Amen!

God bless you all!

Paul Huggins